Training Your Dog

A Day-by-Day Program

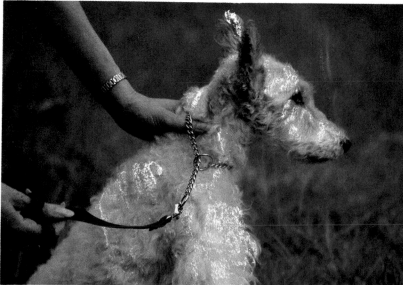

Kathleen Berman
& Bill Landesman

Sterling Publishing Co., Inc. New York

This book is dedicated
to all those dog owners who love their pets enough
to want to train them.

Library of Congress Cataloging-in-Publication Data

Berman, Kathleen.
  Training your dog : a day-by-day program / Kathleen Berman & Bill
Landesman.
    p.   cm.
  Includes index.
  ISBN 0-8069-0576-X
  1. Dogs—Training. I. Landesman, Bill. II. Title.
SF431.B435 1994
636.7'0887—dc20   93-44536
                                                             CIP

10 9 8 7 6 5 4 3

Published by Sterling Publishing Company, Inc.
387 Park Avenue South, New York, N.Y. 10016
©1994 by Kathleen Berman and Bill Landesman
Distributed in Canada by Sterling Publishing
c/o Canadian Manda Group, P.O. Box 920, Station U
Toronto, Ontario, Canada M8Z 5P9
Distributed in Great Britain and Europe by Cassell PLC
Villiers House, 41/47 Strand, London WC2N 5JE, England
Distributed in Australia by Capricorn Link (Australia) Pty Ltd.
P.O. Box 6651, Baulkham Hills, Business Centre, NSW 2153, Australia
Manufactured in the United States of America
All rights reserved

Sterling   ISBN 0-8069-0576-X

Dedication

When all you have is gone
And all who love you have left
He still remains faithful.
His loyalty reaches beyond the barrier of time.
His affection and respect cannot be bought but must be
    earned.
He cannot be bribed by food
As can all other animals, proving their inferiority to him.
You are everything to him
His life centers around you
Your praise is his greatest gift
Your scorn his deepest sorrow.
Ready to serve you at any time
He is only too eager and willing to prove it.
Glad to defend you against any odds
He will give his life for yours
Without your ever asking.

He would jump willingly into the fires of hell
Just to be there with you.
Ready, he stands at your side,
Like his ancestors have done before him.
And his offspring will do after him.
Whether gently playing with your children
Or guarding your mate with his life
He does his job well.
With an understanding almost superhuman
He has only one fault
And that is—someday
He will break your heart
For dogs live only a little while
And in a few quick years
He must say—good-bye.

Bill Landesman

The bond of complete trust between author Kathy Berman and her companion Sigie is evident here. So much of what dogs give their owners cannot be put into words. This photo says it all!

Contents

Introduction

Running loose and heading for a heavily travelled street, a dog stops abruptly, drops down, and waits when his owner raises a hand and commands, "down." This simple command and his ability to follow it have probably saved the dog's life.

Instead of scrambling out into traffic when his owner opens the car door, a dog lies down on the backseat as he is commanded and is spared the deadly dangers of the street.

A police dog who has chased and cornered a criminal prepares to attack. The man, however, has given up. The handler calls the dog, who quickly returns to his side, sparing the criminal needless injury.

A woman tells her dog to "heel" and quickly walks away with him, preventing a confrontation with another bigger, more aggressive dog.

These are some examples of the importance of obedience training for dogs, which can prevent your dog's injury or death and protect others as well. The obedience-trained dog is a superior dog who in times of emergency or distraction can ignore the distraction and function according to the training he has received.

Besides being far less accident-prone, an obedience-trained dog is a happier dog and leads a more interesting life than his constrained counterparts. He can accompany his owners to places where untrained dogs could not. For example, there is no longer any reason to leave the dog behind when it's time for a family outing. He can be depended upon to obey commands and to stay with the family.

Another important reason for obedience training is to increase the communication between owner and dog. When a dog defecates or urinates in the house when left alone and is beaten by his owners when they return, it is evident that little understanding or communication exists. Obedience training, which in this case would include a housebreaking routine, helps the dog and the owner to each understand the needs of the other.

Even if a dog has only a basic level of obedience training that consists of just five commands on leash, he or she has a vocabulary of eight or nine words, one of which is the all-important word "no." The beginning of communication and understanding is present. At a high level of obedience training, when a dog can perform twenty or thirty commands off-leash during distractions, the dog has a vocabulary of almost fifty words. It is then improbable that there can ever be a misunderstanding between this dog and his owner. Their communication is at a maximum.

Showing the dog his proper place in the scheme of things and his relationship with his family and the world are other important reasons for obedience training. Not knowing your place in life can be very confusing. Imagine an employee on a new job not knowing which of the people he works with are his superiors and which are not. He is unsure of himself and uncertain from whom he should take orders. Only when these relationships are properly explained can he begin to function smoothly. Obedience training shows the dog his proper function and clearly establishes the authority of his owner.

Obedience training also temporarily fuses the dog and his owner into a single working unit. When working on obedience routines, their minds function together, each knowing what the other is thinking. They become a team, a team that is successful only when both dog and handler perform correctly. A dog cannot follow commands that are not given properly. Therefore, proper handling is most important. A trained dog given to an unknowledgeable handler will not work well, if at all.

This team spirit cannot be achieved by allowing a dog to sleep in your bed, hugging and kissing a dog, or by giving him treats. The only way to achieve it is by obedience training. As you both work on the routine, you function mentally and physically as one; it soon becomes your dog and you against the world of distractions.

An ideal way for an owner to train his dog is to do it himself. The advantage of this approach is that it helps develop maximum respect between the owner and his dog, since the owner is the sole handler throughout training. Using a good training manual such as this one increases greatly the chances of success.

Be aware that there are important differences in training dogs for the specific purpose of showing them in the obedience ring and training dogs for practical, everyday conditions. Books aimed at the obedience ring may not teach you to bring your dog up properly and how to correct problem behavior like barking and chewing.

When training your dog, choose a manual written by a professional trainer that covers the type of training you want your dog to have. Also, be aware that coordination, endless patience, the ability to follow written instructions, and the daily time needed to work with the dog are prerequisites for training him. If you obedience-train your dog diligently and consistently, you will be very pleased with the results. Training will create a bond of respect that will infinitely increase your joy in dog ownership and your dog's joy in his environment. It's a happy ending well worth the time invested.

Kathleen Berman
Bill Landesman

Kathy and Sigie demonstrate a strong working relationship. Their eye contact and body language is direct and respectful.

What Kind of Dog Should You Choose?

Choosing a puppy is always a joyful experience, but, if tempered with good judgment, this transient joy will become a lasting pleasure for all concerned. The noblest treasure you can receive from your dog is an abiding love and respect that can provide a lifeline in an indifferent, sometimes hostile world. This love and respect is achieved through mutual responsibility, and it is for the enrichment of your union that you convey to your dog the boundaries of behavior expected from him.

Now that you have been flushed with the poetry of purpose, we must become practical. If you are unable to walk your dog, for any reason, on a regular basis, or if it is impractical for you to be saddled to the daily routine of his elimination outside of the home, then perhaps you should consider a dog that can be completely paper-trained. It is unusual, and often confusing to a dog, to expect him to relieve himself on paper sometimes and outside on other occasions. However, it is possible to have it both ways, if this is your decision, and if you are gone eight hours or more daily. The choice should be made by you beforehand as to whether your pup will be paper-trained or housebroken. As we will see throughout the entire training procedure, consistency is the single most important element in conveying to your pet what is expected of him and in defining the boundaries of behavior beyond which you will not allow him to transgress.

Assuming that your decision is to paper-train your dog, you will find one of the smaller breeds preferable. A paper-trained Saint Bernard or Great Dane might strain an otherwise amicable relationship with you and your garbage man, unless you could train the dog to flush his own waste down the toilet.

Among the smaller breeds, you must further select one that will not chew your household possessions into pieces. Many dogs, when left alone, make a vocation of chewing everything accessible, not from spite, as most people allow themselves to believe, but from anxiety. All dogs have anxiety as to whether their masters will return, but those with the greatest apprehension chew the most. A breed such as the toy poodle or Shetland sheepdog will produce a diminutive stool and will not be excessively anxious when left alone.

When we discuss chewing, we are not including pups up to six months of age. All puppies chew. This is perfectly normal because they are teething. If the dog is older than six months and is still chewing, you must determine whether he is a chronic masticator.

If you are unable to walk your dog and refuse to have him paper-trained, then the only alternative is to have him eliminate in a confined area in your yard. Do not let the dog off the leash in the street. Not only is this unlawful, but it is very dangerous for your dog. Since a dog is totally dependent upon you for his welfare, you should be aware of your responsibility for his well-being. Anyone who can't or won't make this commitment should not have a dog. A cat or bird can be a sane compromise in such a situation.

If you have children or a very busy household, you need a dog that is not inordinately high-strung. A good candidate would be a big, calm dog, one that might have to take physical abuse from children. An example of a big dog that can take abuse from children without getting hurt or becoming aggressive would be a standard poodle, Labrador, golden retriever, English setter, Great Dane, Saint Bernard, or Great Pyrenees.

If your dog is going to be left alone for long periods of time during the day, you would not want to get one of the hunting breeds. A similarly bad choice would be some of the Northern breeds (Northern breeds are dogs bred for cold climates). They can all be notoriously heavy chewers. For this reason, again, you should probably opt for one of the calmer breeds or a more moderate-size dog such as a good shepherd or Doberman. (A good dog is one that is not nervous, aggressive, or shy, and does not have any of the numerous negative characteristics that are found through indiscriminate inbreeding in the puppy mills.)

If the dog is not going to be left alone all day, and you have children, then you'll want a friendly, docile dog. You could consider one of the hunting breeds or a good German shepherd. What you want to avoid with a lot of children is a small dog like a toy poodle, schnauzer, Maltese, Yorkshire terrier, or Chihuahua that is going to have to defend himself against pinching, poking, and pulling little hands. These dogs are quick to retaliate by nipping and biting. Such a situation is torture for the dog and dangerous for the child.

As far as obedience training for competition, or to achieve competence on working-dog level (working dogs are dogs bred to be worked, such as to control sheep), some of the finest dogs for this work are Dobermans, good shepherds, golden retrievers, standard poodles, Rottweilers (with the right owners), Labradors, and many other dogs if they are brought up properly, with a respectful attitude towards their owners.

A dog such as the standard poodle would be very good for competition and can achieve the highest level of obedience possible, as can a Doberman or good shepherd. Not only are these dogs highly intelligent, but the desire to please is so great that they can reach the zenith of their capabilities in a surprisingly short time, with skillful training.

Dogs reflect the temperaments of their owners, and nervous, high-strung people will have nervous, high-strung dogs, even if the dog is intrinsically a calm one. Erratic behavior by the owner increases apprehension in the dog and can possibly lead to a serious behavior mistake such as biting. When people in a household are arguing, the animal will often try to find refuge in a corner, away from the scene of the argument. If a husband and wife or parent and child engage in physical aggression such as slapping or pushing, the dog will usually try to stop the stronger one. Just as your dog has the perception to realize that he must play more gently with little people (babies and younger children) and women, he instinctively comes to their defense against an aggressor, whom he realizes is out to harm his family. People who are hypertensive and very erratic should try, whenever possible, to tone down this negative behavior for the mental stability of their dog. In addition, they should overcompensate by buying a dog with a very calm temperament: a Saint Bernard, Great Pyrenees, or Great Dane. A Doberman, schnauzer, or hound such as a German short-haired pointer would be quicker to bite, since they get agitated more quickly. The following chapter contains additional information that you will find helpful when considering a dog.

Two dogs in the same family can and should work side by side with their owners. Alex and Samantha cooperate with their trainers Kathy and Bill in this respect.

9

Home Environment and Personality Factors

Apartment Versus Private Dwelling

If your apartment happens to be a walk-up, you might decide to get a small- to medium-size dog that could be totally paper-trained. If you decide on housebreaking your puppy, he will have to relieve himself about six times a day, gradually tapering to three or four outings as he attains adulthood and gains maximum control over his excretory functions. But rejoice for your pet: he will consider these outings as the high points of his day. To a dog, nothing is more fun than the sights, sounds, and smells of the great outdoors.

Living in an apartment, in close proximity to neighbors, you must have great concern not to disturb them with noise. A dog that barks and howls all day long while you are out working is sure to bring the neighbors' wrath against you. A dog that is at ease when left alone will not bark and howl as much. These problems would not be quite as crucial in a private home since you are not in such close proximity to your neighbors.

For the apartment dwellers who are also working people, we would preclude most of the hunting and northern breeds and some terriers, as they are infamous for their chewing and barking. Note that living in the apartment is not the only reason why they behave as they do. It is the owner's all-day absence that creates the anxiety and its attendant problems. Dogs that would not be anxious if left alone in an apartment for a long period of time are German shepherds, Dobermans, Saint Bernards, Great Danes, bullmastiffs, mastiffs, Great Pyrenees, poodles, Labradors, golden retrievers, dachshunds, and Shetland sheepdogs.

Country Versus City Dogs

Larger breeds of dog could be chosen to live in the country, where there is plenty of space. They can be the hyperenergetic hunting-breed types such as the Irish setter, Chesapeake Bay retriever, German shorthaired pointer, weimaraner, or vizsla. This type of dog will remain quietly sedate and companionable in the evening after romping in a spacious backyard all day. However, if it is left at home alone for long periods, the close confinement will increase his apprehension to the point where he will feast on your household contents.

If choosing a city dog, a smaller breed of dog will prove preferable. Many of them require no auxiliary exercise other than that which they get from roaming about the home, which is advantageous if they have to be left alone for many hours. (A word of caution for urban dwellers: games like go-and-fetch-it can be fatal on city streets.)

A large dog can be a city dog if it has a calm temperament. Examples of such dogs are a good German shepherd, Saint Bernard, Great Pyrenees, Great Dane, mastiff, or Labrador. These dogs are all very good with children and are placid, nondestructive types when left alone.

The Childless Couple

This may be a business or professional couple who have a busy life and are seldom home. Such a couple needs a pet that is content to be left alone all day, not one whose nerves will compel him to chomp their nearly completed master's thesis into confetti. They would also be wise to choose a dog that requires minimal exercise. Being greeted by a pet ready for a hundred-yard dash is quite disconcerting, especially after you've been through an exhausting day at work.

The Elderly Couple

You have been through enough trials and tribulations in your lifetime. Now your time has come to enjoy each other and a new member who will provide a joyful addition to your quiet household. Foremost, you don't want a dog that will require you to puppy-sit on week-ends! Next, you need one that you are physically able to handle, not only for walking, but to maintain control over in obedience work. Dogs that will prove ideal include Italian greyhounds, Yorkshires, or toy poodles.

Grandparents are notorious for indulging their grand-children. Please do not allow this well-intentioned behavior to carry over to your dog. You might want to consider buying a dog of some five or six months. House-breaking and chewing problems are minimized at this age, the dog's temperament is pretty well formed, and the dog can often be purchased at a more reasonable price. Mixed breeds could also be considered.

The Family with Children

Your pet is not a wind-up toy that can be pounced upon and ridden to exhaustion or pulled apart and recon-structed again. You cannot remedy abuse with the tight-ening of a few loose screws. We know that you realize all this, but the problem is conveying it to the children, that inexhaustible group of little people who always seem to have the energy we wish we had. A big, calm dog, or even one of the hunting breeds, would be ideal for this situation. In this environment, a dog must be big enough to withstand physical abuse comfortably and calm enough to accept it graciously.

The Single Woman

The single woman requires a dog that won't be jealous of her gentlemen callers. The dog will probably have to accept many new people coming and going. It can't be aggressive, or excessively pesky. It can be small or large depending upon your preference, but a big, calm dog can serve the purpose of protection as well as compan-ionship should you ever need it. The man who came to dinner and wants to stay all night would never be put off by a toy poodle, but will listen when a Great Dane speaks. Also, important consideration must be given to where to put your pet when you wish to be alone with your boyfriend without his suffering rejection syndrome. Some dogs couldn't care less in what pleasures you in-dulge. If your dog is such a dog, he can be left in the room. If, however, he shows an uncanny interest in your private moments, then give him a bone and relegate him to another room in the house.

If you have a very small dog and have been making a cradle of your lap for him most of the time, it will be very difficult for the dog to accept sharing you with anyone else. This situation can be a setup for aggressive, jealous behavior, so watch carefully for it.

The Senior Citizen

The senior citizen usually has specific needs that differ from the younger couple. Often, climbing up and down stairs or taking daily walks would not be practical. They have neither the strength nor the need for a very large dog. A small-to-medium-size breed that can be totally paper trained and is content with a relatively sedentary life would be the ideal choice. It could be a six-month-old purebred dog or a mixed breed, if carefully chosen. This minimizes housebreaking and chewing problems and cost. The older the dog gets, the less desirable he is considered, only because most people want very young puppies. A dog that would chew or bark when left alone could be fine in this situation. Terriers and small hunt-ing breeds can be a good choice, as is a toy or miniature poodle. A bichon frize, Chihuahua, Shih Tzu, dachs-hund, Lhasa apso, Maltese, or West Highland white terrier could also be very good. Stay away from shep-herds, Dobermans, huskies, pointers, and Labradors; if they happen to be excessively exuberant or strong-willed they will be difficult to control.

The Permissive Owner

The permissive owner is the type of person who loves his dog too much to correct it. His kind indulgence becomes a disaster when he needs to get control of his own pet. This type of person feels that if you reason with your dog the dog will quickly learn to follow your commands. Such people embrace the philosophy that all dogs really want to please their masters!

In truth, dogs are as varied in personality and moti-vation as people. Some will respond to your demands for the sheer pleasure of your praise. Many others will obey only because of severe enforcement of the commands. Army and police attack dogs and seeing-eye dogs are reliable because they fall into this second approach to training. So we have two basic obedience attitudes: the dog that obeys if and when it wants to and the one that obeys because it has to. Those that fall into the former group will doubtless have occasions when they will con-test your demands. The proper approach to obedience work will ultimately propel your pet into the latter cat-egory.

The only way obedience can be real at any level of distraction is when the dog knows he responds to your command because he must. Your dog's reliability could save one or both of your lives some day. That is the ultimate reward of control.

When you obedience-train your dog you are teaching him that he can never defy you and get away with it. Make absolutely certain that no laxity on your part shows him differently. The way to ensure this is through consistency. If you withhold firm physical correction, you are preventing your dog from experiencing the justifiable consequences of his negative actions. Only by experiencing such consequences will bad habits be discontinued and good ones encouraged.

If you give your dog the choice between correction and praise for a given action, he will make the right decision. No dog enjoys an atmosphere of nebulous demands. Boundaries that are clearly drawn and consistent make a dog happy and secure.

The Show-Off

Most of us are familiar with this basically insecure type of person who almost without exception selects a shepherd, Doberman, or Rottweiler as his ego extension. These breeds have a reputation for being very smart and easy to train. They also make excellent guard dogs and command a certain awe and respect when walked down the street. Sir Show-off uses his dog to embellish his ego, and very often beats the animal into temporary submission, rationalizing that he is showing the dog who is boss! Little does he realize that he is playing the role of agitator and will shortly find himself in a confrontation with the dog's mouth. A dog that is hit by his master will usually eventually turn on him. He should not receive punishment that manifests itself as physical abuse!

Dobermans and Rottweilers have much less tolerance for unjust treatment than most other dogs. Consequently, these breeds have been saddled with a bad reputation for turning on their masters. The best suggestions I would have for Sir Show-off would be to get a life-size picture of the breed of his choice and a six-foot bullwhip. It is a most practical means of keeping both man and dog out of trouble.

The Society Couple

The society couple is used to lots of entertaining. A

These Shar-Pei pups—Rex, Edward G, and Laverne—are in a safe, clean, enclosed playpen with lots of safe toys they can play with. Puppies are always adorable, but rearing them is serious, full-time work.

calm, even-tempered dog that can accept chaos in the home without becoming agitated and that will not chew when left alone is what is needed in this situation. Probably a small-to-medium-size dog, such as a poodle, Maltese, and even some of the terrier breeds, would be a good choice.

The Confirmed Bachelor

The pet for the confirmed bachelor must be content to be left alone all day and prepared for lots of action at night. It is important that your pet not be so rambunctious when you arrive home as to intimidate your lady friends into a quick departure. (If you are a passive type and prefer being pursued, you might want to select a member of the retriever breeds. He may bring you home a real prize!) Stay away from the anxiety chewers or your romantic pad may become a garbage dump overnight. Also, avoid overly aggressive and protective dogs, unless you plan on remaining a bachelor for the rest of your life.

The Traveller

The traveller is used to hitting the road with great frequency. If you are a traveller, whether for business or aesthetic reasons, you'll need a compatible travelling companion. Select your travelling companion from among the calm, nonchewing dogs such as the shepherd, Saint Bernard, Great Pyrenees, where space permits, or even a golden retriever. Any dog should be initiated into the travelling routine fairly early, such as learning the commands "sit," "stay," and "down" in the car. We will refer to training in the car later on in this book.

The Young Married Couple Planning a Family

Since you have a serious commitment planned for the near future with ample challenges to face when the stork drops his bundle of joy into your eager arms, you'll need to select a dog with the proper temperament for the household. You are going to have a furry friend for eight to sixteen years of your life, so it is very important not to be frivolous in your choice. Your pet must make comfortable adjustments to the addition of new members and to their growth in size and personality. The breed you

choose must be good with children. If you are home all day and expect a child soon, you can pick from among the hunting breeds, which are nervous when left alone but wonderful with children. A small dog of terrier or toy class may not be good, for they don't tolerate children well and tend to nip. A dog from the working class such as the Bouvier des Flandres, boxer, Great Dane, shepherd, or Saint Bernard makes an excellent choice for a family situation, and can be left alone without chewing problems if both husband and wife work outside the home. Also, the family is protected for some time in the future.

There are many cute and medium-sized breeds such as Kathy's Shar-Pei, named Ralph Kramden, which can offer companionship as well as protection for a woman who is alone.

13

Where to Find Your Dog

When you have decided upon a suitable breed for your personal or your family's situation, the next step is looking for the breed of your choice in appropriate places. You can find wonderful dogs anywhere, as you can poor-quality dogs. The three main sources are breeders, pet shops, and animal shelters. A breeder sells specific breeds, while a pet shop has one or two of a variety of breeds.

When looking for a dog, you must learn to assess general levels of health and soundness of temperament. If a dog looks sickly, no matter what the source, it is time to shop elsewhere, or you are in for a lot of headache. Also, selecting a dog from a breeder or pet shop with a favorable reputation and one willing to give referrals is always a positive approach. Any worthwhile breeder or pet shop should be happy to refer you to its satisfied customers. A breeder or pet shop that has been around a long time is appealing.

When visiting a breeder or pet shop, observe the premises. They should be clean. Puppies have to be clean to be healthy. Dirty premises breed disease. Dogs should have fresh food and clean water, and their papers should be cleaned often. All the dogs should look perky and healthy. The breeder or owner of the pet shop should be knowledgeable and helpful. He or she should be willing to take the time to answer your questions, and should be just as helpful after the sale as before. There should be a health guarantee subject to a veterinarian's inspection. There is so much competition in puppy sales these days that you can afford to be discerning about the best choice.

Price can be a gauge of quality or of fad. Don't expect that just because you pay more, you are inevitably getting a better-quality dog, or that because the price is more moderate, the quality of the dog is compromised. Pricing has so much to do with overhead, regional economy, popularity of breed, availability of breed, sizes of litters, supply as relates to demand, and a host of other factors.

There are many conscientious breeders out there, as well as a host of fine pet shops. People and businesses who sell puppies without conscience and integrity will usually not be in business for very long. Their reputation will return to haunt them. There is no long-term profit to be made in sleazy pet sales. Look around, compare, ask a lot of questions, and then choose the breeder or pet shop.

You can get a dog from a shelter, newspaper ad, an animal league, and by finding a lost dog in the street with no identification tag. All of these are admirable ways of getting a pet, and perhaps saving a dog's life. Usually, however, you will have less background knowledge of the dog. Its emotional and physical health are unknown quantities. What this means is that you may end up spending more money at the veterinarian's office, or for professional training, than you might have spent for a pup at a breeder's or pet shop; but everything can still turn out wonderfully when all is said and done.

The decision of where to buy is not simple or foolproof. However, if we look carefully and use some common sense, rather than just responding emotionally, we are likely to make a fine choice regardless of where we go. But choose we will, and we will be all the richer for it. For in this life, few people experience the fulfillment of unconditional love possible with a dog.

Choosing Your Dog Through Observation and Testing

What a dog becomes is inextricably related to what his parents are; so, in testing and evaluating the dog, you should actually be more thorough in assessing the parents' traits than those of the pups, though both are very important.

When you go to the breeder, chances are that one or both of the parents will be there. The first thing you should do is watch the reaction of the adult dogs. How do they react to you when you walk into the house? Most probably you will see the mother. Is she afraid? Does she back away growling, or just retreat shyly? Does she try to bite you, making an all-out attack for no reason? Does she bark without restraint, or try to shower you with licks of love? Or, does she just look at you, come over to smell you, and then walk away, while keeping a dignified eye on you? This last behavior pattern would be the ideal reaction should you be looking for a guard dog, but it is also very desirable behavior for any type of dog. The superfriendly parent could also make a good guard dog or be wonderful with children. The fact that she is not afraid could qualify her for guard work, and she should not be discounted simply because she is overfriendly.

The dog that backs away, afraid, growling, and cowering, would not make a good guard dog. It may have been beaten up or abused. If a dog makes an all-out attack on you, find out his background. Has he been hit? This dog's puppies might possibly qualify for guard work, but would have to be tested further.

It should be noted that the mother may be slightly overprotective and nervous because her puppies are there and she sees strangers in the house. She may appear fearful or aggressive, but this may be simply because she wants to protect her young. If you are not sure that this is the cause, she must be tested in another area all by herself.

The dog that lies on the floor, ignoring you completely, possibly asleep, should not be considered as a guard dog. This dog, can, however, probably be a good pet, although chances are he won't learn obedience too well.

Note how the parent dogs walk up and down stairs. Walking on a flat surface can sometimes hide physical defects such as hip dysplasia. Take note that you are testing the parents, not the puppies, so far.

If you are looking for a dog for guard work, ask the owner to take the parent dog outside, quietly remove the leash, turn, and walk away. This is a responsibility test for the dog. Does the dog acknowledge his owner's presence? Does he maintain proximity or stay in the general area close to the owner? Does he sniff, run around, and "make" (eliminate waste) while simultaneously looking back at the owner? If the answer is yes, then you may have a dog that would qualify for the kind of responsibility that guard work entails. If the dog shows disinterest in the owner's whereabouts, and tends to take off, you had better look somewhere else.

Many breeders who are negotiating a sale with you will not let their dogs take a test. They will give you all kinds of excuses that range from leash laws to "The dog has no training." Don't succumb to these babblings; look somewhere else.

The ultimate test of a guard dog is courage. You could have the owner walk along with the parent dog on a leash, and suddenly a professional trainer could jump out and make loud threatening noises, and gestures, shoot a cap pistol in the air and observe the dog's reaction, or even bang a garbage can cover against a wall as he advances threateningly, yelling at the same time. If the dog tries to attack him, but was friendly before, it will make an excellent guard dog. If it jumps up at him licking and wanting to be friends, you have further testing to do. At least the dog is not afraid. If she backs away and growls, she might be able to protect you, and is worth further testing. If she is afraid and cowers behind her master, she and her puppies are not suitable for guard work. You must look elsewhere. Make sure a professional performs this test. If you try it, you may find a good guard dog but may not live to enjoy his company.

Vicious dogs do not make good guard dogs. They are overly aggressive and beyond the owner's control. Usually, they must be put away in a cellar or some other place of confinement when people come to the door, because they cannot be trusted not to bite. A dog can't offer you any worthwhile protection unless he can be with you in situations of potential danger. A good guard dog is a very controllable dog that knows when to react through your command, or on his own, but only to unfriendly, threatening people.

Once you have decided the parents are okay, the next step is to pick your puppy from the litter. When doing this, test the puppy first to make sure it can hear and see and is able to walk around. Clap your hands, whistle, quietly open a door, and suddenly yell "no" to the puppy. Does he get moderately or excessively afraid? Push your hands close to the puppy's face, back and forth in a wavelike motion. Is he hand shy? Why? Has he been hit? If parent and puppy are both afraid, and they haven't been hit, it may indicate that it's not a "learned" condition. See if the puppy will walk with you as you pull him gently on a leash. Call him and see if he will come to you. In general, see if he is alert and lively. Look at the eyes and make sure they are clear, not clouded and drippy. Look at the ears. They should be clean, not waxy and odorous. Try to see the consistency of his stool, which will indicate if he has worms.

The degree of importance attached to the testing of your dog would be determined by the requirements you set for him. Should you want a "working" or guard dog, testing is extremely important for determining behavior traits. If your only requirement is a pet for the family, then less critical evaluation would be required on temperament. However, you would want to be painstakingly meticulous in testing the dog's health and physical characteristics. Minutes spent on testing can save months of frustrating problems later on.

Paper-Training Your Dog

The best time to take your puppy home is when he is approximately eight to twelve weeks old. He should be taken to the veterinarian immediately and checked out thoroughly. Your agreement with whomever you purchased the dog from should be contingent upon the dog's perfect health; if the dog is not in perfect health, you should be entitled to an immediate refund or exchange. This agreement should be in writing. A handshake is a friendly gesture, but doesn't mean much when a battle of rights ensues.

As a general rule, keep your puppy away from other dogs and places where other dogs have urinated or defecated. He can pick up diseases from these sources very quickly because he is very young and vulnerable. The ideal place to initiate your dog's excretory functions would be an enclosed backyard that no other dogs can get into.

You will have to paper-train for an initial period, until the time you can convert to housebreaking. This period could last from one to four weeks. Choose the area in which you would like him to "make" (defecate or urinate). Preferably, this should be a small room. Put papers down, covering the entire floor surface.

Right after the dog eats, place him on the papers. Clean up the first elimination, reserving one newspaper to retain the scent. This will now be placed on top of a fresh pile of newspapers. A dog's sense of smell is seven times more powerful than that of a human, so he will be able to locate his spot from that one newspaper, even though the smell eludes you. Repeat this process of conserving one newspaper until your dog zeros in on one particular area where he has gone again and again. Never use a suppository on your dog for purposes of housebreaking or paper training.

Gradually reduce the papered area in size, until it is only as big as necessary for your dog. This may be as small as one foot square for a small toy-class dog.

An eight-week- to six-month-old puppy should be fed three or four meals a day. Leave the food out for ten minutes only. Give him as much water as he will drink, but only at the times indicated in Table 1. Table 2 is a typical puppy schedule for a couple who both work.

Table 1. Schedule for eight-week-to-six-month-old puppy

Time	Instructions
6:50 A.M. (or first thing in morning)	Put dog on papers
7:00 A.M.	Food and water
7:10 A.M.	Put dog on papers
10:30 A.M.	Food and water
10:40 A.M.	Put dog on papers
1:00 P.M.	Food and water (dogs under three months get fourth meal at this time)
1:10 P.M.	Put dog on papers
4:00 P.M.	Food and water
4:10 P.M.	Put dog on papers
7:00 P.M.	Water; put dog on papers
9:00 P.M.	Water; put dog on papers
11:30 P.M.	Put dog on papers, no water

If you decide to continue paper training for the life of the dog, then follow the schedule for six-months-and-older dogs. If not, as soon as your puppy can go outside, switch to the housebreaking routine and schedule.

Six-months-and-older dogs should be fed two meals a day. This is preferable to giving them one big meal that they will gulp all at once. Give your dog all the water it will drink, but only at the times indicated. The schedule for a six-months-or-older dog is shown in Table 3.

In cases where three meals are necessary, as with dogs under five months old, an 8:00 P.M. feeding and 8:10 P.M. placement on papers can be added to the above schedule.

If your dog makes a mistake in another area of the house, use a specially designed deodorizer for this purpose that can be obtained from pet stores or suppliers. No commercial cleaner such as bleach, ammonia, pine disinfectants, or novelty sprays will work. The dog's nose knows the difference, and he will find his spot again and again, much to your chagrin.

Catching Your Dog in the Act

Since it would be useless to snap a picture and take your dog to court with it, you must find another means of conveying to him what is expected. He must be watched constantly. Keep him in whatever room you are in, and attach a piece of clothesline about three or four feet long to him. This will facilitate his easy removal from a favorite retreat under the couch or behind the bathroom bowl and will allow you to promptly transfer him to the newspapers. When you see your dog trying to make in an undesignated area, yell NO loudly and lead him with the clothesline right onto the papers. When he finishes making on the papers, praise him by saying, GOOD BOY. The contrast between NO and GOOD BOY shows your dog what is expected of him.

If your dog still does not make on the papers, then just watch him closely again. The next time he attempts elimination in the wrong place, yell NO again and quickly lead him back to the papers. Repeat this process

Table 2. Puppy schedule for a working couple

Time	Instructions
6:50 A.M. (or fist thing in the morning)	Put dog on papers
7:00 A.M.	Food and water
7:10 A.M.	Put dog on papers
8:30 A.M.	Water; put dog on papers.
5:30 P.M.	Food and water
5:40 P.M.	Put dog on papers
9:00 P.M.	Water; put dog on papers
11:30 P.M.	Put dog on papers

Table 3. Schedule for six-months-or-older dog

Time	Instructions
6:50 A.M. (or first thing in the morning)	Put dog on papers
7:00 A.M.	Food and water
7:10 A.M.	Put dog on papers
11:00 A.M.	Water; put dog on papers
3:30 P.M.	Food and water
3:40 P.M.	Put dog on papers
7:00 P.M.	Water; put dog on papers
11:30 P.M.	Put dog on papers

over and over until the mistakes are eliminated. Do not hit your dog, rub his nose in his feces or urine, or yell SHAME. These are all exercises in futility. Continue to deodorize all mistakes with the aforementioned product, and do not show your dog the exasperation you are bound to feel at times in this training process. He will sense your weakness and use it against you. Also, do not shake a can filled with marbles, pebbles, etc., at your dog as a correction. This will only make your dog neurotic and cause him to be afraid of loud noises for the rest of his life.

During the night, and when you cannot be with your puppy, you must confine him to a small room or part of a room with a gate enclosure, so that he can see out and doesn't become claustrophobic. He will not be excessively anxious, because he can see out. The kitchen is probably the best place, because you have a tile floor that can easily be deodorized. Never confine the dog to a carpeted area. It is much more difficult to remove the scent from carpet and more attractive for him to make on the carpet.

When you are out, you may place your dog in a small room, perhaps again the kitchen, and cover one half of the room with newspapers. Any mistakes found upon your return that are not on the newspapers should be deodorized immediately. Do not yell NO to your dog upon returning home. He will not know what he is being corrected for. Just put a clothesline on him and watch him. *Never leave anything on your dog's neck when you are not at home.*

Do not bother to correct your dog for making off the papers, even if only two or three minutes have passed.

Just clean up the mistake and begin watching him again. Your dog can only understand a correction when he is caught in the act. He must only be corrected at that time.

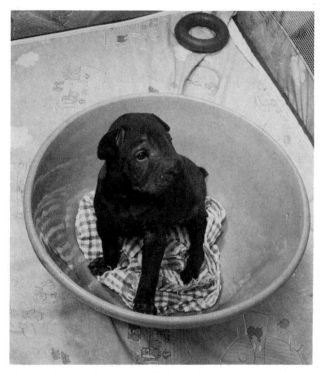

Shirley "bowls" us over! Kathy's little puppy Shirley is too young to abide by any housebreaking or paper-training rules. Pups four weeks old should relieve themselves in the safe confines of a washable playpen, but this will change as they get a bit older.

Housebreaking the Puppy

When you housebreak a dog, you break the dog of the habit of relieving himself indoors. A housebroken dog only "makes" outside. In contrast, a dog that is paper-trained eliminates his waste exclusively on papers in a designated area in the home.

For housebreaking purposes, a good-quality dry food is preferable, except in rare cases where it causes persistent diarrhea. Normally, dehydrated packaged burgers or other dry-packaged food will make the dog drink large quantities of water, creating the urge to urinate constantly. Keep the dog on dry food which agrees with him. (See Table 4 for ratio of meal to size.)

At the times designated on the schedule, allow the dog as much water as he wants, but only at those times. Always take him out right after eating or drinking. Keep him out for five to ten minutes, not longer, during this housebreaking period. You want him to know what he is out for. Half-hour romps around the block will only confuse him. If he doesn't "make" in that time, fine; bring him in and watch him.

A dog over six months of age would be put on a similar schedule. Let him eat twice a day, eliminating the middle meal, but keeping the water schedule that has him going out about every three to three and a half hours. If

Table 4.

Age	Size of Dog	Meal
Weaning to 3 Months (4 Meals a Day)	Small breeds	¼ cup of dry dog food
	Medium breeds	⅓ cup of dry dog food
	Large breeds	½ cup of dry dog food
	Very large breeds	½–¾ cup of dry dog food
3 to 6 Months (3 Meals a Day)	Small breeds	½ cup of dry dog food
	Medium breeds	¾ cup of dry dog food
	Large breeds	1 cup of dry dog food
	Very large breeds	1½ cups of dry dog food
Over 6 Months (2 Meals a Day)	Small breeds	½ cup of dry dog food
	Medium breeds	¾–1 cup of dry dog food
	Large breeds	2 cups of dry dog food
	Very large breeds	2–4 cups of dry dog food

you feed and walk him as indicated, confine him overnight and when you can't be with him, catch him in the act of making and deodorize the area, the dog will be housebroken in about two weeks.

All quantities are approximations. Check with the veterinarian and the breeder and observe the dog. If he's getting too fat, you are feeding him too much. If he is not gaining weight properly, feed him more.

The Schedule

Table 5 shows the schedule for a three-month-old puppy eating three times a day. Leave the food down for ten minutes only.

For dogs six months and older, the 11:30 A.M. feeding can be eliminated. The last solid food will have to be given at the 11:30 P.M. walk, approximately six hours after eating. This way, you will be producing an empty dog and, if no water is given after 9:30 P.M., a dry dog also. At all other times, between walks, the dog should be watched closely. He should be in whatever room you are in, and should be dragging three to four feet of cotton clothesline knotted on a bolt snap and attached to his collar. This will give you a handle with which to grab the dog if he starts to make a mistake in the house. When this occurs, yell NO and drag him right outside to finish making. As he makes, praise him and bring him back into the house, continuing to watch him. If he doesn't make outside within five to ten minutes, bring him back in the house and continue watching him. The dog should not go outside to run around and have fun during the housebreaking period. It will create confusion in his mind and delay housekeeping results.

Always have your dog drag the clothesline when you are able to watch him. If you have to spend time looking for the leash and collar, by the time you get them on him he won't know what he is being corrected for or why he is being taken outside. Also, don't correct him unless you catch him in the act. Should you be distracted sometime and a mistake occur, firmly resist the temptation to scream at and scold your dog and rub his nose in it. Just clean it up and forget about it.

For times when you are not able to watch your dog or be with him, such as during the night or on a short shopping trip, the dog must be confined. This consists of using two gates to confine the dog in a space not much larger than he is himself. The dog will not make if he has to lie in his elimination; this is his introduction to learning to control himself.

Gates are the preferred method of restricting your dog to a small area. The confinement should be very close without the dog feeling alienated from the household. He should be able to look out through the gate and feel he is a part of the action, while learning to restrain himself. Should he make a mistake, he will be wearing it. If the area of confinement is too large, it is possible for him to make in one area and lie down and sleep in another, and this he will do. Confinement should be on a hard tile floor that can be deodorized thoroughly. An absorbent rug is much more attractive to a dog and can never be completely deodorized. He tends to make less on a smooth, hard surface.

Your dog should be able to control his bodily functions for eight hours by 3½ months of age, and certainly for an hour or two as you go marketing or to visit a friend. Don't let your pet get in the habit of signalling to you when he would like to go out. Some dogs will do this every hour on the hour. You can easily be fooled into thinking this is a legitimate request that would result in a mistake if not indulged promptly. What you don't know is that a dog can always squeeze out a few impressive drops once he has discovered that this is the way to get outside for some fun and frolic. If this particular ploy is allowed to blossom into a full-time routine, you may

	Time	Instructions
Table 5.	7:55 A.M. (or first thing in the morning)	Take him for a fast walk so he will urinate.
	8:00 A.M.	Food and water
	8:10 A.M.	Walk (5 to 10 minutes on the leash, only to make)
	11:30 A.M.	Food and water
	11:40 A.M.	Walk
	3:30 P.M.	Food and water (last solid food of the day)
	3:40 P.M.	Walk
	7:00 P.M.	Water and walk
	9:30 P.M.	Water and walk
	11:30 P.M.	Walk (no water)

come to feel like you're constantly on call, ready to ease the plight of a doggie in distress.

Some dogs will continue to eliminate even after you yell NO and start dragging them outside. Don't let this deter you. Drag him completely outside, even if there is nothing left. Then praise him with the words GOOD BOY and take him back in the house again. This will end the training exercise on a positive note. If you do not get him outside, the housebreaking will take longer. Ideally, you should try to catch your dog as he starts walking in circles, and startle him with a loud NO before he begins to eliminate.

Confinement, watching the dog, catching the dog in the act, and the feeding-walking schedule should housebreak a dog in about two weeks. In that length of time, the dog will be making once or twice in the house for the entire first week, but things will be pretty well under control as soon as the whole routine is underway. A liquid deodorizer such as Nilodor® should be used in a very strong solution of 15 drops to three cups of water. This mixture should be stored in a jar and used over and over again as needed. No commercial bleaches, pine cleaners, or sprays will work, because even if you can't smell the odor anymore, your dog certainly will. As long as he can smell his past mistakes, his nose will lead him back to these spots to repeat the experience. Nilodor has a very clean, fresh smell that does not mask odors but actually eliminates them.

If you are a working couple and no one is home during the day, housebreaking will take longer. It can take a month to six weeks and even more, because during the day you can't confine the dog to a very small area. Having the run of a large area like the kitchen, he will be able to make in one end of the room and sleep in another, without wearing his mistake. Ground gained when you are home will be lost when you aren't. Otherwise, all else on the schedule will remain the same.

It is a good idea to walk the dog as soon as you get home, before feeding him. This walk should be very short, approximately two minutes, like the first walk in the morning. People who complain that they walk their dog for an hour outside and that he makes inside upon returning are allowing this to happen by taking walks that are far too long and then not watching the dog when he returns.

This housebreaking routine is successful because if your dog isn't allowed to make in the house because you are watching him, and won't make in confinement because he doesn't want to wear it, there are only two choices left: make outside, or burst. And we haven't witnessed any explosions yet.

In cases where walking a dog is not possible, for whatever reason, paper-training must be chosen as the alternative to housebreaking. Paper-training, as explained in the previous chapter, means that the dog will make on papers placed in one particular area inside the house.

Paper-training is similar to housebreaking in that the schedule of feedings remains the same, but instead of walking your dog outside, you put him on the newspapers. The papers, in the initial stages, take up the entire floor of a small room. Later, the area is narrowed down to as little as a foot square, depending on the size of the dog.

The confinement area will initially consist of an entire room covered with the papers. Instead of closing the door, use a gate to confine your dog in the room. After five days and a few mistakes off the papers, remove the papers covering half the room and deodorize the exposed area with a very strong solution of Nilodor. All other areas in the home where mistakes occur should be thoroughly deodorized as well.

In addition to placing your dog in the room with the papers as a correction each time he tries to make elsewhere in the house, confine him in that room at night. As fewer mistakes are made, usually in about five days to a week, the dog will not require overnight confinement anymore. The dog must have access to this room at all times; gate him in when no one is able to watch him, such as when you are asleep or out. Make sure that every time the dog makes on the papers you lavishly praise him.

Correcting Fear and Aggression through Obedience Training

We can speak extensively about the role of diet in fostering a healthy mind as well as body. (See next chapter.) Proper nutrition alone will allow for clarification of thought, an increased attention span, an increase in memory, and an improved nervous system. It will *not*, however correct any fears a dog has concerning garbage cans, vacuum cleaners, firecrackers, people, newspapers, guns, being left alone, being confined, being hit, or being abused. These are all personality and behavioral problems which can only be overcome by working them through with obedience training.

The typical person will try to deny that his dog has any fears, aggressions, and other idiosyncrasies. For example, when a dog tries to climb over a wall because he fears the sound of firecrackers, we pick him/her up in our arms, cuddle him, and say, "big, bad noise—you go away." Our behavior is doing everything to confirm the fears and not a thing to overcome them.

If a dog doesn't like or is suspicious of people, it is because either he hasn't been exposed much to them, and so has not developed any basic discernment, or has had bad experiences with some people and becomes more highly suspicious to the point sometimes of aggression. The owner in this position usually resolves the problem in this way: every time someone comes to the home, the dog is locked in the basement, kitchen, backyard, bedroom or bathroom. The dog is put anywhere and everywhere except where he should be—with people.

Another common problem occurs when the dog destroys items in the home or chews on the carpets or furniture. The typical person will confine the dog or throw him out in the backyard. He will never recognize the dog's need to chew and the responsibility on his part to sublimate the chewing desire towards some constructive and acceptable goals.

There are many more behavioral problems that dog owners do not bother to correct. For example, dogs are afraid of the vacuum cleaner. The noise and movement make them fearful; they either run away from it, barking and growling, or try to attack it. Dog owners will attempt to resolve this problem by vacuuming when the dog is out for a walk or out in the backyard or in any other way that does not deal with correcting the behavior.

Dogs are also afraid of the garbage truck which comes by in the morning. The dog will dart away uncontrollably, pulling you down the street with him. If it is a big dog, you have a real safety problem, in terms of yourself and him. But with any size dog, the uncontrollable fast movement is always dangerous. What do we do to solve this problem? We walk the dog in the backyard, or we wait till the garbageman has made his pickup and then we walk the dog in front, watching cautiously for any other larger vehicles which might fly by, scaring the senses out of him.

The last example we will use is the car ride. Your dog, much to your chagrin, is not an ideal car companion. He can have any of several reactions: vomiting, urinating, or defecating in the car; jumping around wildly in the car, obscuring your vision and creating a very dangerous situation; salivating all over the windows, seats, and your clothes; or simply gnawing on the upholstery or other parts of the car. Any one of these reactions is enough to discourage most people from repeating the car ride. The dog will never ride in the car again unless there is a dire emergency! As with all the common examples we have discussed above, this is the wrong approach. Not only is the dog owner not correcting the problem, he is ensuring that in future similar circumstances, the dog's behavior will be even worse. In the next section, we will consider the appropriate obedience exercises to correct these specific behaviors.

The Roles of Nutrition and Specific Obedience Exercises in Behavior Modification

Behavior problems should always be approached with proper nutrition, which means the best-quality pet food you can find, and then, where appropriate, specific obedience exercises. The following chapters provide very detailed instructions on initiating and completing each command. Color illustrations throughout this book depict these procedures.

The basic premise involved in general obedience training and specific work in trouble areas is to diffuse the problem by training the dog to concentrate on something else. That something else is obedience commands worked specifically for the purpose of splitting the dog's attention between fear, etc., and the absolute requirement of obeying the owner's commands. If the commands are given wisely, fairly, and appropriately, the dog in his learning to listen to and obey them will, on his own, come to realize that the thing feared is indeed not so fearful after all. We are providing a structured substitute for the fear, instead of allowing it to flourish unchecked. No amount of cuddling, hitting, screaming, or locking the dog away will ever overcome the problem. These will simply foster more feverish behavior.

You may be saying at this point, "So what if my dog is afraid of garbage cans, garbage trucks, or loud noises, people, guns, or vacuum cleaners? We just won't expose him to any." Your dog, when given a choice, is a very socially oriented creature. He does not wish to be cloistered away from the real world. He is unhappy being afraid, just as people are miserable when they are afraid.

Fear, as with people, engenders erratic behavior. Fearful people are thoroughly unpredictable. So are dogs. The primary behavior trait which evolves out of a dog's fear is biting. When the biting is precipitated by fear, it is called fear-biting. But let there be no mistake about it: A fear bite hurts just as much as an aggression bite. So it is up to the owner to mould the dog's mind and behavior constructively, so the dog will live a happy, well-socialized, fearless life.

You may be saying, "So what if he does bite? He is so small, it couldn't hurt that much. And besides, he's not very likely to bite me, just other people." It should be

pointed out that biting is not the only problem your fearful dog may suffer. Your dog can develop many preventable medical problems because of his fear. These will cost you a small fortune to keep under control if you can, since they are mentally and not biologically induced. Among the list of medical problems which can plague your dog are vomiting, diarrhea, constipation, urinary incontinence, poor digestion, gastric bloat, mucoid colitis, nervous system disorders, lick granulomas, asthma, bronchitis, self-mutilation, pancreatitis, and, ultimately, cancer.

Let us take each problem outlined in the previous section, one by one, and structure some basic exercises to offset the negative behavior and build the confidence of the dog. Fear of firecrackers is far too common among dogs of many breeds and sizes, not just small dogs. Hearing sensitivity is so acute in dogs that what may irritate us is intensely annoying and fearsome to dogs. When the noises occur, first try acting normal, as if everything is just fine. Show this to your dog through your voice intonation, body posture, and choice of activities. If you show fear of the firecrackers, the dog's fear will intensify.

Next, teach the dog to heel, at an unstressed time, and automatically sit and stay. Using these well-learned commands, pick up the leash and begin to heel the dog, requiring automatic sits at frequent intervals. Do some stays, but not for too long. Keep the dog moving and distracted with the obedience routine. You will work it at other times also, to keep the dog in shape. You will be amazed at how the noises gradually become insignificant to the dog.

The next exercise is directed to the dog traumatized or mistreated by people, the dog who is unsocialized. All people are suspect to him. He has high anxiety over meeting anyone. He may back away and cower, back away a safe distance and bark, jump all over the people, or even try to bite.

Do not let people greet a dog fearful of strangers or even a very friendly one with overwhelming exuberance. Dogs like to meet and assess people on their own terms. They prefer to make the first move. It is better to pet them under the chest than on their heads; the latter move looks very threatening. Don't make fast, jerky, aggressive moves and don't push yourself on him if he's not interested in being petted. Let him sniff you. Walk into a room normally and sit down. Relax and allow him time to observe and assess.

As the owner of a dog fearful of strangers, your responsibility is to teach your dog to heel at the door, on leash, whenever anyone comes; this requires an automatic sit and stay at heel position. The dog cannot indulge his whim or aberrant behavior while he is under your command. If he becomes somewhat relaxed, you can then release him with OKAY, and allow him to make friends with the stranger.

Another problem dog owners face is anxiety or sublimation chewing and destruction in the home. It is disheartening to us as trainers to see how many people deny the dog's need to chew. They chastise him for chewing the wrong things, but rarely think of redirecting him to the proper things to chew. First, run out and purchase natural sterilized bones and Nylabone® and Cressite® rubber toys. Get several sizes and shapes of each. Avoid rawhide or delicate squeeze toys, your socks, old blankets, stuffed dolls, old shoes, etc. Present these toys to your dog as his own. Bring them around into each room he is in with you. Any toys which he is not particularly interested in should be rubbed with cheese, chicken, bacon grease, or other tantalizing substances to make them enticing. When he chews on the wrong things, yell NO sharply, and when he stops, offer him his own toys as you praise him with GOOD BOY. You are training this dog in elementary obedience. Work him in all rooms of the house. Every room he is worked in he will feel secure in. If you keep him out of rooms where he can be supervised, you will build up his destructive anxiety, and your worst fears will be confirmed.

The noise and movement of vacuum cleaners make dogs fearful of them. Since vacuum cleaners are used in almost all households, the dog should be taught to overcome his fear. Develop your dog to a level where he can heel and automatically sit, stay, and down-stay. (All these commands are described in subsequent chapters.) Begin to work him in the room on heeling and auto-sits, away from the person vacuuming, but still close enough where he can see and hear the vacuum. Walk and work him towards and away from it. When he is a little more relaxed, try some sit-stays at the full six feet of leash. As he really becomes confident, drop him into a down-stay. He feels more vulnerable in this position.

Never make aggressive moves with the vacuum cleaner. Never get too close to him with it. Work small, short sessions over a period of days. First, get him to heel and automatically sit. Next, try sit-stays. Finally, use the down-stays. You will have built up confidence to the point where his fear is a thing of the past.

Loud trucks, especially garbage trucks that are backing in, will wreak havoc with your dog's sensibilities. Build the dog up to the point where he knows heeling, auto-sits, sit-stays at a distance, and recalls. Work him at quiet times, along the familiar area, in all these commands. Be ready for the time when the truck arrives. Your dog must be well schooled before this.

Work auto-sit with heeling, stopping at frequent intervals. Be ready to correct the dog hard if he runs away or does not sit when you stop. The sits are automatic, so he must watch when you stop. He can, at the beginning, be looking at the truck instead of you, but he must sit while he is doing it. Gradually, he will watch you over all the other distractions. Try gradually some sit-stays at six feet. Then try some recalls, with you standing near the distraction and calling him to sit and stay in front of you, until a new command is given. If you were to do the recall away from the distraction, it would not be as useful, since your dog would be only too happy to run away from it. In fact, he would probably be running right on past you if you do not reel him in tightly in front of you, commanding him to sit.

The last problem we will treat with obedience exercises is the dog's behavior in the automobile. This can be far more serious than firecrackers and vacuum cleaners. It must be dealt with positively and intelligently. It should be obvious to people, but it is not, that many dogs will be fearful of cars, if all they represent is a visit to the veterinarian, the groomer, or the boarding kennel. If only stressful experiences occur subsequent to the car ride, your dog is justified in being anxious every time he is forced to ride in the car. How do we make car riding pleasant for him? Easy. We take him on many short trips to pleasant places—rides to get a newspaper, rides to grandma's house, rides to go to the bank, rides to meet "daddy" at the station. All these experiences have very pleasant connotations and the dog will relax in the car. He will be able to handle the occasional trip to the veterinarian because so many positive experiences have been confirmed.

Dogs that vomit in cars have usually been fed too soon before the ride. Feed your dog a good three hours before and two hours after the ride. It will also minimize the urination and defecation. The more frequently the dog vomits, urinates, or defecates, the more the dog will associate getting sick with the car ride. Bring toys in the car, and leave the dog for short periods where you can watch him. Come back and drive home. Don't leave him for long periods unsupervised so heavy anxiety can develop with its subsequent destruction. Short, frequent trips to pleasant places is the key.

Train your dog in basic heeling, auto-sit, and stay, including the down-stay. When he is proficient, work him towards the car. Command him to sit and stay at heel position. Open the door. Correct him severely if he lunges for the car or into it. He must be controllable. Dogs belong in the backseat, not the front, and they should not be jumping to and fro. Release your dog into the backseat, with the release word OKAY, and then tell your dog to DOWN-STAY. Walk him to the passenger's side, and then command him to DOWN-STAY again. Then get in the car. Release him again with a quiet OKAY, if your dog is calm, or keep him in down-stay longer.

When you are ready to get out, use the commands DOWN and STAY again. Get out. Go to the passenger's side. Open the door and take the leash. Your dog is still obeying the commands DOWN and STAY inside the car. Wait a few moments, and then release him with OKAY. If the dog is extremely excitable, command him with a DOWN-STAY for the entire ride.

The Counter-Effects of Bribing Your Dog

There are so-called "professional" trainers who use a biscuit-popping technique to attempt to correct certain behavior in puppies. This technique basically consists of bribing the dog with biscuits. Practitioners of this misguided technique decry punishment or corrections with a choke collar, claiming they are cruel. Tragically, some people unfamiliar with dogs may fail to see the difference between a dog doing a trick in a quiet room for a cookie or a piece of cheese and the training of dogs to ensure favorable conduct even during distractions or emergencies, possibly when the dog is not even hungry! A dog who loves to bite the mailman will indulge in this behavior, ignoring the cheese or tidbit. He usually ends up as an incorrigible offender, another victim of those who tried to bribe him with food.

When real professional dog trainers (such as those who train seeing-eye guard dogs, police dogs, and those trainers who work for the American Kennel Club) train dogs, the equipment they begin with is a metal choke-chain collar and a canvas or leather six-foot leash. Cheese and cookies would be laughable to them. Real dog trainers know that intelligent dogs rarely want to please people whom they do not respect. They would never want to deprive the dog of his right to learn by making a mistake and experiencing its logical consequences and his satisfaction when he is praised for correcting his mistake.

Part of the harm done by the food-bribing technique is that it robs the dog of the birthright of all God's creatures, that is, the right to the consequences of his own actions. He will always be able to more clearly understand the difference between punishment and reward than the concept involved in bribing him with food.

Author Bill Landesman and Dream. The proper equipment for training includes a six-foot web leash and a chain collar. Observe how Bill and Dream are looking at each other. This is teamwork, based on love and respect. The attention from a dog such as Dream can never be achieved through food bribing, but only through positive training techniques, which imbue in the dog the desire to please the handler.

Nutritional Supplements

Proper nutrition can be obtained through foods and also through supplements. For those who want to know what supplements are available on the market in order to keep their pets healthy and retard the aging process, here is a list of some of those more widely used, and what they do:

Vitamin C

Vitamin C is an antioxidant, which means it conserves the body's use of oxygen. Oxygen is needed in all life processes. We require aerobic (with oxygen) activity for cardiovascular health. Anaerobic environments are environments that do not have oxygen. Cancer cells grow in an anaerobic environment. Anything that builds up oxygen in the cells helps to replenish them. These cells are regenerated. Anything that robs oxygen induces the more rapid death and slower replacement of cells; the poor-quality newer cells have deranged coding blueprints.

Vitamin C helps build the entire immune system without harming vital bacteria, enzymes, etc. It regulates the formation of intercellular substances having collagen. Collagen is a cement-like material which holds together all the cells in your body. It helps make bones and cartilage strong. It is also a painkiller. The C Complex consists of vitamin C as ascorbic acid and bioflavonoids (also known as vitamin P), which occur largely in the whites of citrus fruits. You can get vitamin C or vitamin C complex from rose hips, or vitamin C from acerola berries.

Vitamin C also comes in a fat-soluble form called ascorbyl palmitate. Fat-soluble C can have greater effectiveness in preventing fat peroxidation. Most forms of vitamin C are water-soluble. Ascorbyl palmitate has a greater effect on the lipid structures of the brain, heart, and central nervous system, protecting these organs from harmful free-radical buildup. (Free radicals are byproducts of cell metabolism and cause the cells to die more quickly than normal.) Ascorbyl crystals can be sprinkled in food for easy daily use.

There is another form of vitamin C often used by veterinarians, called sodium ascorbate. This is a buffered form of vitamin C, which means its reaction in the body is alkaline. This is essential when vitamin C is used intravenously, directly into the circulation. The bloodstream is alkaline, and vitamin C if injected in an acid form would have fatal effects. But veterinarians all know the proper form to inject, and you would only be administering oral doses.

Sodium ascorbate in powdered form is used widely by holistic veterinarians, because it is less likely to irritate the stomach or produce diarrhea in very large quantities. You can also get the buffered form, known as calcium ascorbate. In this way, you would not be getting too much sodium.

To give you some guidelines as to how much vitamin C to use for your pet, let us take the experience of a real pioneer in vitamin C research, Wendell O. Belfield, D.V.M. He has addressed the issue of hip dysplasia with remarkable results. He recommends that a certain amount of vitamin C be given to dogs daily. The amount varies according to the size of the dog. It should be as follows: for small dogs, 500 to 1,500 milligrams daily; for medium dogs, 1,500 to 3,000 milligrams daily; for large dogs, 3,000 to 6,000 milligrams daily; and for giant dogs, 6,000 to 7,500 milligrams daily. This dosage is based on normal daily preventative use. The amounts would be increased for seriously ill or severely stressed dogs and very often augmented with intravenous injections of sodium ascorbate for faster effects, at sometimes as much as ½ gram per pound of body weight. It would be up to a veterinarian to decide upon such megadoses.

You won't find vitamin C in your average pet multivitamin, because manufacturers still erroneously believe that dogs manufacture a suitable amount of their own vitamin C. Though dogs do have the capability innately to manufacture C, unlike us humans, the reality is that, because of increased stress, poor nutrition, lack of proper exercise, etc., most dogs manufacture *far less* vitamin C than they actually require, and so they constantly need supplements. Some dogs don't manufacture any vitamin C at all.

Dr. Belfield also has a program of vitamin C treatment which was successful in the complete prevention of hip dysplasia in eight litters of German shepherds with parents who had hip dysplasia or had produced offspring who developed hip dysplasia. The pregnant bitch is maintained throughout the pregnancy on anywhere from two to four grams of sodium ascorbate daily. Increased amounts are given for giant breeds. Beginning at birth, puppies are maintained on a liquid form of ascorbate such as CE-VI-SOL® by Mead Johnson, at 50 to 100 milligrams orally daily. When the dogs are between three weeks and four months old, instead of liquid ascorbate they are given ½ gram of sodium ascorbate powder daily, depending upon size. After the four months, the dosage for all dogs is increased to one to two grams daily, until they are two years old. This program is certainly worth a try at any stage of a dog's life, whether it is diagnosed dysplastic or not, since vitamin C has multitudinous other benefits.

Vitamin A

Vitamin A is a fat-soluble vitamin essential to healthy skin, heart, respiration, immune system, eyes, mucus membranes, red blood cells, etc. Vitamin A is an antioxidant, helps to deactivate harmful free radicals, acts as an anti-tumor agent, accelerates repair and new growth of tissue, and aids vision. There is a water-soluble form of vitamin A called beta-carotene.

The beta-carotene in dry form is more stable than in the oil form, where it can oxidize in the presence of other lipids (fats). Veterinarians will often use the water-soluble form of vitamin A because it is not stored in the body and because very high levels of up to 200,000 units daily can be used to fight severe infections quickly, without harmful results. You could never use close to that amount of a toxic drug without killing an animal.

Vitamin A is used to treat cancers because it helps the immune system and detoxifies poisons. Corneal ulcers have been helped when a solution of vitamins A and E has been applied directly into the eye. Vitamin A is also used to treat conjunctivitis and other eye infections. Nutrition-oriented veterinarians use high doses of vitamins as part of a program of good nutrition and also to treat canine and feline distemper, feline leukemia, heart problems, kennel cough, bronchitis, parvo virus, skin ulcers, and many other disorders.

Vitamin E

Vitamin E is also a fat-soluble vitamin that plays beneficial roles in the reproductive, nervous, and vascular systems. It is also applied topically to burns, and prevents scarring. Vitamin E comes commonly in doses of 200, 400, and higher international units (IU's). You can get this vitamin as alpha tocopherol or in its more complete form of mixed tocopherols. When you purchase alpha

tocopherol or mixed tocopherols, there will be a letter D before the name on the bottle to signify that it came from a natural source. If the letters DL appear, then it is synthetically produced, which is more economical.

We maintain our pets on daily doses of from 200 IU's for small dogs and cats up to 800 IU's daily for larger animals. We spread it topically on burns, abrasions, and ulcerations. We will sometimes mix vitamin E with aloe gel to gain the best benefits of both. Natural or synthetic, vitamin E should be a daily part of your pet's regime.

Vitamins C and E are often used in natural pet foods as preservatives and antioxidants instead of BHA and BHT, which are more commonly used. Veterinarians use vitamin E to treat hair loss, arthritis, cancer, cataracts, respiratory disorders, circulatory disorders, eye ulcers, bladder inflammations, slipped discs, skin ulcers, pustules and acne, pregnancy disorders, virility disorders in males, parvo distemper, and heart conditions. Wheat-germ oil is a natural form of vitamin E, but it must be used quickly or it can turn rancid. When wheat-germ oil spoils, it tastes bitter. You may be better off using the gelatine capsules, which protect against rancidity.

Super Oxide Dismutase

Super Oxide Dismutase (SOD) is an enzyme supplement which is used to retard aging. SOD occurs naturally in the body as a protein enzyme dismutase. The dismutases attach to harmful free radicals and deactivate or dismutate them.

As the animals get older, they lose substantial amounts of these valuable SOD enzymes. External supplements of SOD are a very good option, for many reasons. One reason is that slow aging is associated with high SOD levels in the body, and rapid aging is associated with low SOD levels. This substance can help to slow down the aging process and prevent or reverse many degenerative diseases.

SOD has also been used in cancer research. Injectable SOD was infused into tumors in hamsters, increasing their survival time. SOD reduces cell death significantly in the toxic effects of radiation.

Superoxides are a significant key to cancer therapy. Superoxides are destructive free radicals formed during aerobic metabolism. In research done on 50 different cancers at the University of Iowa and Wabash College, all were found to break down the cellular defense mechanisms of these superoxides.

Arthritis sufferers have been greatly relieved when treated with SOD, which reduces swelling. Orgotein is the human injectable form of SOD, used safely and effectively in relieving morning stiffness, pain, and swollen joints in about 85% of patients. Oral tablets of SOD are available in 2,000-unit doses. These can be used for animals as well. The injectable form for your animal is called Palosein®. Ask your vet about Palosein.

SOD can also be administered to your pet in the form of sublingual liquids, liquids administered under the tongue. This pleasant-tasting liquid form can be more easily absorbed than tablets. There is reduced cost, in terms of frequency of veterinarian visits for shots (which are also very effective).

The SOD sublingual is called formula 3000 SAFE-GUARD Sublingual SOD. It is manufactured by Bricker Labs, 18722 Santee Lane, Valley Center, California 92082. Bricker Labs also carries the sublingual male and female formulas, as well as thymus only, adrenal only, and a natural safe-growth steroid.

Vitamin B_{12}
Vitamin B_{12} is also called cobalamin, due the cobalt centralized in the B_{12} molecule. Neither man nor animal can synthesize B_{12}. Bacteria and fungi manufacture this within the intestine. B_{12} regenerates red blood cells and the central nervous system. It prevents anemia, stimulates energy and appetite, and increases memory and learning ability. It acts as a coenzyme for increased utilization of the proteins, fats, and carbohydrates, and can also be taken in the sublingual form for maximum utilization.

B_{12} is assessed in terms of micrograms, not grams or milligrams, of international units. An average human daily dose would be 500 mcg. Use this quantity as a relative guide for your dog, according to the size of the animal. The same company that manufactures SOD—Bricker Labs, Valley Center, California—also manufactures sublingual liquid B_{12} as well as B_{12} lozenges. Holistic vets use B_{12} to combat feline leukemia and other wasting diseases such as cancer and severe anemia. The B_{12} is used to increase the red blood count.

Vitamin B_{15}
Vitamin B_{15} is another vitamin used to slow down aging. It conserves the body's use of oxygen and is used by veterinarians in treating heart problems, circulatory disease, emphysema, liver degeneration, and premature aging. The most popular form used for several decades in Russia is called Aangamik-15. This can be obtained at a local health food store.

B_{15} also comes in drops, which are used to arrest the growth of cataracts on a dog's eyes. The drops are called TRUE-15 Optique. They are manufactured by American Biologics, 111 Ellis Street, Suite 300, San Francisco, California 94102.

There is a serious depletion of B_{15} in processed pet foods. All kinds of melon seeds are plentiful in this nutrient, but you should juice the seeds along with the flesh and, in the case of watermelons, the rinds.

Vitamin B_{17}
Vitamin B_{17} contains amygdalin, which is used in the treatment of cancer. B_{17} is found in foods such as grains, apple seeds, apricot pits, peach pits, and bitter almonds. B_{17} is more centralized in the pits nowadays, whereas years ago some B_{17} could be found in the flesh of the fruits also. Commercial farming has depleted this nutrient and many other essential nutrients from the soil. If it is not in the soil, how can it be in the fruits and vegetables that grow in that soil? Our produce is only as rich as the soil it grows in.

B_{17} can be taken in foods that contain it, in tablets, or through injectables given by your veterinarian. Laetrile is the drug form of B_{17} that is being used by veterinarians to treat cancer, distemper, and feline leukemia. In cancer therapy, Laetrile, unlike chemo-therapeutic agents, affects only the diseased cells.

Dr. John Craige, D.V.M. in Sherman Oaks, California, is the foremost proponent of the use of Laetrile in veterinary medicine. He suggests that one teaspoon of ground-up apricot pits be given daily to dogs that weigh up to 50 pounds. The pits should be ground up just before they are used. A 25-pound dog would use half the dosage, and so on.

Laetrile is a positive synergist, with vitamin C boosting its effectiveness in building the immune system. It also acts as an anodyne (pain reliever), no small factor in treating disease. Laetrile is drawn to the cancer cells, which contain beta-glucosidase, and kills only them. The cyanide in Laetrile destroys the cancer cells without destroying healthy tissue.

Laetrile must not be overused or soaked in liquid, which could break down and release the cyanide. Use Laetrile under the supervision of a veterinarian conversant with its use, its forms, and the quantities that will produce maximum benefits. B_{17} is a nutrient that not only slows down the aging process, but is also significant in cancer treatment and control. The incidence of cancer in our pets is increasing. We owe it to them to seriously investigate any nutrient that is significant in treating cancer.

L-Cysteine
L-Cysteine is another nutrient that slows down the aging process. It is an amino acid that is also an antioxidant, and helps protect against bacteria, viruses, chemicals, and radiation. L-Cysteine is contained in eggs, garlic, onions, cabbage, and muscle meats. It is also available in supplements of 500 to 2,000 milligrams per day.

Basic Obedience for Puppies (Three to Six Months Old)

There is a need to establish communication between you and your puppy. Even though you cannot demand very much from your dog, so far as expecting him to respond to complicated commands, you must retain enough control over him to be able to live together amicably.

The equipment you will need to begin basic obedience training with your pup consists of a metal chain-type collar and a six-foot leather or canvas-web training leash (Illus. 1-5). Use this equipment for his daily housebreaking walks, to familiarize him with it, and to eliminate any fear that may carry over into the obedience training. Puppies should be taught obedience training for 15 minutes a day, no longer. Some pups can only tolerate short training sessions; their attention wanders or they get very nervous. For this type, five-minute segments, two or three times daily, will work better than one 15-minute session.

Commands

Come

You need some way of mobilizing your dog into action. If you can't get him to walk with you, he can't be taught the SIT-STAY command or any other command. The word OKAY is used to start the dog moving. This is followed by the dog's name—in this example, Joe—and the command COME. That combination of words—"Okay, Joe—Come"—will enable you to start the dog walking with you on a leash (Illus. 6-8). This is not an exercise in heeling; it is a prelude to the command HEEL, which will be taught to your dog when it grows older. The COME command will sound like this: OKAY, JOE—COME.

The first obedience routine will consist of walking back and forth in a room and stopping approximately every six feet. Do not start this training out of doors, where distractions will be intensified, making it very difficult for your pup to concentrate. Try to work in a minimally furnished room where you will not be tripping over table legs or bumping into couches. Another reason for working in a minimally furnished room is that if there is a lot of furniture, your pup can draw emotional support if he is allowed to lean on or get under it. Work him in the middle of the room, as far from furniture as possible. You are initiating your dog into moving with you, not defying an obstacle course.

In many homes, training the family pet becomes a joint family venture and a favorite spectator sport for the children and their little friends. Cheers from the crowd and sage remarks from the peanut gallery do not a good training session make. Resist the temptation to make a public spectacle of yourself and a fiasco of the training sessions.

Sit

You will begin placing your dog on sit immediately, with the first training session, using the techniques that follow. Walk back and forth, making only right about-turns with your pup, giving the command OKAY, JOE—COME! as you begin the walk. When you stop, place your dog on a sit by pushing down on the dog's rear end with your left hand, while drawing up smoothly on the leash with your right hand (Illus. 9). Say the word SIT only once. As your dog is forced to sit, you will praise him by saying GOOD BOY. As you give the command SIT, physically push the dog into the sit position. Give only one command. This should be repeated for some five to ten minutes every day for about a week. After that time your puppy should be able to sit for you on command, especially in the house, without distractions.

Illus. 1. The correct equipment for training your puppy consists of a metal chain collar and a six-foot leather- or canvas-web or nylon leash.

Illus. 2. The correct way to install a chain collar. Slip the chain shaped like the letter P over your dog's head, as you face him.

Illus. 3. A side view of the correct collar installation.

Never reward him with food or he will not work without it. Your physical and verbal praise will be his complete reward.

After your puppy has been placed on the command SIT for about a week, he should be sitting most, if not all, of the time on your command. If he will not sit all of the time, you can now start correcting him. It is safe to assume he knows what you want. If he refuses to heed your command to sit, you can now correct him by giving a slight jerk on the leash, accompanied by the word NO (Illus. 10), and then praise when he sits (Illus. 11). The proper leash correction consists of a quick jerk and re-lease movement, *not* an extended hanging. If he still does not sit, give another correction and then the SIT command again. Keep this up as long as necessary, until he sits, alternating the correction with a new SIT com-mand. Do not go back to placing your dog on the com-mand SIT once you have decided that he knows the command. Only correct him in the manner described above.

If you are wondering how hard you should jerk your dog when correcting him, the answer is simple: His ac-tions will tell you. If he refuses to sit after a few correc-tions, it means you are correcting too lightly. If he sits after a correction, then you know that the correction was adequate.

The greatest cruelty a misguided handler can inflict on a dog is an ineffective under-correction. Under-correcting encourages further resistance and the need for many more corrections, which all add up to a lot of unnecessary pain for your dog. A hard, effective correc-tion will do the job the first time, ending the need for any further corrections. The biggest injustice to a dog is dis-pensed by the misguided "kind" person who is too good-hearted to jerk his dog. This same kind person, three months later, gives the uncontrollable dog away to the dog pound. Such a person is a dog's greatest enemy.

Stay

Begin teaching your dog the command STAY only after your dog will reliably sit on command for you. When your dog is sitting, hold your left hand extended in front of him, slowly moving it towards his face, your fingers pointed downwards (Illus. 12). Say the word STAY only once. Hesitate for two or three seconds and then praise him. On the next stop, once your dog has sat, give the STAY command accompanied by the hand signal. It is important to note that you should give only one STAY command and signal.

After about five repetitions, give the STAY command when he sits, and then turn and face your dog. Return quickly to the dog's side and praise him. The stays should be so short at the beginning that the dog doesn't have a chance to break. This will end the routine on a positive note, with your dog being praised.

Next, repeat the SIT and STAY commands five times, and step back away from your dog about two feet. Im-mediately drop your hand, return to your dog, and praise him. That is enough for the first day.

Gradually increase the distance between you and the dog as you back away to the full six-foot length of the leash (Illus. 12–15). Always return quickly before your dog has a chance to break. Correspondingly increase the time until, after about a week, your dog can sit and stay for half a minute at the full length of the six-foot leash.

After an additional week of practice, your dog should be able to stay for a minute despite slight distractions. If your dog breaks the stay by getting up, the correction should be NO, with a slight jerk on the leash from the full six feet away (Illus. 16) and a repetition of the com-mands SIT and STAY (Illus. 17), together with the cor-rect hand signal. Don't wait until your pup runs to you. Try to correct him as he breaks the stay. Should he get far, drag him back quickly to the point where he was first told to stay, and give a new SIT and STAY command (Illus. 18) with the hand signal. Leave your dog again. Should he get up and break the stay upon your return, give him the usual NO correction with a jerk on the leash and a repetition of the commands SIT and STAY with the proper hand signal.

Continue this until you can return to his side and praise him without his breaking. Moving slowly, when returning to your dog, will help him to hold the stay (Illus. 19). Hesitate for about three seconds after return-ing to the dog's side before praising him (Illus. 20). In this way, you will be teaching him to wait for your praise instead of using your mere physical proximity when you return as an automatic release. This hesitation before praising will make the stays much more solid.

Do not expect too much of a three- or four-month-old puppy, and don't put him in a situation where there are severe distractions and you will be forced to correct him frequently. This will make him fearful of the obedience to come later when he will be mentally equipped to handle more intense training.

No

Only one word is going to be used as a correction to convey your disapproval to your dog for some specific wrongdoing. That word is NO.

NO should be used with a simultaneous leash correc-tion that consists of a jerk on the leash with an immediate release. Eventually, NO will also be used verbally only sometimes, after your dog has established a strong association with the accompanying physical correction and there is no longer any leash or line on him.

Do not command your dog DOWN for jumping up on you or at times when he tries to sneak a tasty morsel from the table. Use the word NO for all these negative acts. You should also refrain from lecturing him on proper table manners or on etiquette when meeting people at the door, such as "You know, Poochie, that mommy gets very angry when you take things from the table," or "It's not nice of you to jump on Grandma when she comes to visit." Your dog needs simplification. He wants to know the ground rules. He welcomes consistency because then he will not have to suffer an unjust correction from you when you are in a bad mood and scream at him for doing something you have let him get away with dozens of other times.

NO is a very simple, logical word to use for all negative behavior. It should be accompanied by the proper voice inflection, authoritative as opposed to coy and condescending. And you don't want to go to the opposite extreme and utter a ferocious roar that would turn your dog into a cowering neurotic.

A very important aspect of the NO correction is the praise that should always follow when he stops the behavior you are correcting. If there is no contrast between correction and praise, your dog will not know what he was corrected for. By giving your dog this consistent contrast between the correction on the one hand and the praise on the other, you set the stage for him to make a choice. If you are consistent, he will make the correct choice.

Okay

Just as NO is used as a correction for all negative behavior, OKAY will be used as a release from work or training. Your dog is not a mind reader, so don't expect him to realize when a lesson is over without a verbal release. Likewise, do not expect him to start heeling or sitting simply because you pick up the leash and have it in mind that he should do so. Your dog must be initiated into each training session with a command such as DREAM—HEEL, or WHITEY—COME, and released from work with the word OKAY expressed joyously, to convey to your pet that he is released from control.

Since you determine when a training session starts and finishes, you are also responsible for not overworking your dog to the point of irritability or exhaustion. Several short periods of five to ten minutes are much better than one hour-long marathon.

Illus. 4. The wrong way to install a collar. It is back-wards (reversed letter P).

Illus. 5. A side view of the collar in-stalled backwards.

Illus. 6. Taking up the leash.

Illus. 7. The correct hand positions on the leash.

Illus. 8. OKAY, PUPPY—COME!

Obedience Training at Six Months of Age

Personality Traits

Before beginning to teach a dog basic obedience, it is extremely helpful if you first can assess knowledgeably the dog's basic personality traits. This is because, in following each essential step for learning a specific command, it is almost always necessary to deviate from standard procedure to some extent to deal with your dog's personal reactions to the command.

The scale of basic behavioral classifications includes the classifications overfriendly, high-strung, normal/average, aloof, shy/afraid, fearful biter, and, ultimately, aggressive. A dog can and will travel through these various personality changes, beginning with overfriendliness and then ending favorably by maintaining a normal/average response or ending unfavorably by lapsing into aggression. You can turn an overfriendly dog aggressive, but you can also nurture a normal response in a heretofore aggressive dog. All these refinements are possible with the proper knowledge.

You might rapidly jump to the conclusion that obedience training for your pet is hopeless if, the first time you try to correct him, he bites you on the butt or climbs the leash and ends up in your arms; or, as you start heeling him, he rolls over on his back and obstinately refuses to walk; or, as you start placing him on sits, he responds by curtsying with his front legs and rearing up with his rear. If we only guided you in the corrections for the logical response from the ideal dog, you would be in for a plethora of frustrating times with your pet. Fortunately, there are very few dogs that are actually untrainable.

You have dual objectives at the outset of training. First, define properly and honestly which basic category of behavior your dog justly belongs in, and; second, define and tailor the obedience so that the dog will ultimately gravitate towards the norms, regardless of which

end of the spectrum he started at. The primary value of a professional dog trainer is his acuity to zero in on personality deviations and behavioral problems and to quickly diminish or negate those problems.

We will start by describing the *normal/average dog*. The normal/average dog could be any breed. This dog has probably been in your family since puppyhood. You have most likely not hit him or thrown things at or near him for minor transgressions. He has had a healthy upbringing, untainted by yelling, abuse, or irrational behavior on your part or from any member of the family. He has not been teased unmercifully by little children or left tied up in a cold garage or a wet basement.

The normal/average dog is usually calm and friendly. He does not obey out of fear, but from a genuine desire to please you and gain your acceptance. He cares what you think about him and enjoys your attention. He is not overly excitable with noises, doorbells, or strange people. His behavior is moderate in all areas. He has a well-rounded, stable personality and is the ideal dog for companionship as well as training.

The *overfriendly* dog goes into a frenzy whenever the doorbell rings, as he paces and flies around the room. He trys to lick anyone who is the least bit receptive. His bodily calisthenics resemble a giant springloaded yo-yo that is perpetually overwound. He is the bane of all well-dressed guests, driving many to equal maneuvers around your living room and entrance way in an effort to escape his affection. This embarrassing display is usually stopped when you lock him in the bathroom or an enclosed porch. It takes an extremely long time for the overfriendly dog to calm down, if he does at all. Where the overfriendly dog is large and he jumps up on small children with his paws in their faces, knocking them into walls or off their feet, serious injuries could result.

The *high-strung* dog is an extension of the overfriendly dog. He is very nervous and uptight. He worries about every strange noise. He is likely to react very severely to firecrackers or thunder. You may see visible shaking of his body. The heartbeat may become more rapid. He may try to crawl onto your lap for comfort and security or may cower in a corner away from everyone, shivering. He may whine a lot or howl from fear and anxiety. Colitis is sometimes a related problem, causing momentary diarrhea or acid indigestion. The hair on his back could rise, and he might make a mistake and nip or bite from worry or fear. He overreacts when people come to call. His bark goes far beyond alerting you to someone's presence. He will run around excessively, and often gives your guests a feeling of discomfort at his presence. His behavior makes people reticent about extending their hands to pet him. He might be reacting to you, his master, and his home environment, or his behavior may be a personality trait. Recognizing why he behaves the way he does would be helpful. But it is more important to realize that he behaves in a certain manner, and thereby categorize him for purposes of training efficiency.

The *aloof* dog attempts to do what he wants to do as often as possible. When you attempt to persuade him to obey you, he responds with an attitude that equates with a belligerent child protesting, "Make me." He doesn't work for your praise, only from fear that you will enforce your demands. This rebel is not stupid, as everyone usually thinks. He is smart enough to avoid doing anything that is not absolutely forced upon him. This shouldn't surprise you, because you doubtless know several people who behave much the same way.

The aloof dog can be very lovable at times when nothing is required of him, or he may remain undemonstrative all of the time. He can be stubborn and very hard to housebreak, and is generally unmanageable. Be honest and willing to put your dog in this category if he deserves it. To deny the truth will cause problems all along the way. You will seriously impede training if you follow procedures suited to another type of dog.

The *shy/fearful* dog may have been brought to your home as an adolescent, or even as an adult dog. When a dog has not been in your care for a considerable portion of his life, beyond the eight to ten weeks from birth to complete weaning from its mother, many unfavorable events may have occurred over which you have no control. These events could severely warp your dog's personality. He may have been abused in any number of ways by people entrusted with his care and well-being. These formative months of a dog's life have lasting influence on his mature behavior.

You may be the second or third owner of this dog. In spite of the belief of many people that a dog has absolutely no trouble adjusting to new owners and new environments, this supposition is not true. Many dogs have a great sense of loyalty and emotional attachment to their original owners. They often have difficulty in transferring their affections from one owner to another. Compounding the problem is the fact that many dogs do not go directly from one household into another. The interim period is often spent in an animal shelter, which at best is a very unfriendly, unpleasant place for a dog. When he does arrive in new family surroundings, he has already been somewhat tainted by his feelings of rejection and alienation, and it will take some time before he feels secure in his new situation. The shy/fearful dog has most likely been dealt a rough hand somewhere along the way, and your patience and understanding will go a long way towards overcoming his problems.

The *fearful biter* can be the high-strung dog, the shy-fearful dog, or a combination of both. He acts aggressively at certain times. This is the type of dog that appears vicious and aggressive when at his master's side, but when directly confronted alone, he may back down. His courage also gets a boost when he is surrounded by the protective cover and safety of couches, tables, etc.

A favorite pastime of the fearful biter is attacking people who are trying to leave, or people who merely stand up, touch certain objects, or intrude upon a certain area. This dog looks for an excuse to bite. He especially looks for people who are afraid, thriving on their fear, which intensifies his aggression. His target areas are usually your rump, ankle, or the back of a leg. This is because the fear-biter rarely attacks head-on. He generally prefers making your back his target.

The fearful biter's aggression could be the result of hitting and yelling and other abusive treatment used to correct problems such as housebreaking, jumping, etc., or the result of erratic or irrational behavior on the part of family members. He sees everything out of proportion. An attempt to pet him is often misconstrued as an aggressive, threatening gesture.

The fearful biter progresses in stages from barking to nipping to biting and gets worse as he is allowed to get away with it or is hit for it. He is so overly defensive that he is more apt to make a mistake than dogs in any other category except the aggressive dog. The fearful biter is most dangerous to strangers and, in advanced stages, can be a danger even to his owners and their family members. His behavior can be changed by honest evaluation in placing him in this category and by proper handling methods especially suited to his particular problems.

The *aggressive* dog is the most dangerous and potentially volcanic of all the personality types. He is perfectly willing to bite almost anyone at any time. His presence

Illus. 9. Sit placement. Put downward pressure on your dog with your left hand and upward pressure on the leash with your right hand.

Illus. 10. The sit correction, using the word NO.

Illus. 11. Praise your dog with the words GOOD BOY.

Illus. 12. The hand signal for the stay command.

Illus. 13. Out in front of your dog, putting tension on the leash.

Illus. 14. Out in front of the puppy, putting relaxed tension on the leash.

can be a living nightmare. The aggressive dog will bite on the flimsiest of provocations. He is often loaded with idiosyncrasies, and if he decides that you are threatening his sense of well-being by standing up, blowing your nose, or reaching down to pet him, he will spring into action to convey his displeasure. The aggressive dog's personality may stem from overpermisiveness or from extremely abusive treatment, such as harsh beatings or teasing from children. This damage could have been caused before you got your dog, or your own behavior may be the sole cause of his aggression. If you determine that you are the one to blame, then honestly evaluate what things you are doing wrong and stop them immediately.

However, it is most dangerous for anyone, sometimes even the owner, to work an aggressive dog. You cannot really afford errors in judgment. Indulging yourself in a barrage of excuses is also harmful since you must come to terms with what your dog is and what you are capable of doing to handle this problem and change him. If you feel that this is a challenge beyond your capabilities, consult a professional dog trainer. If your dog passes some of the preliminary tests at the beginning of the following obedience chapters, chances are you can work out his problems with the help of this book. Should he fail these preliminary tests, then professional guidance is definitely called for. Don't chance serious injury to yourself or other innocent people, and don't expose your dog to the possible ultimate necessity of having to be destroyed. We are so conditioned to getting rid of things when they no longer please us that this attitude is often carried over to living things. Even if your dog is aggressive, and you feel you cannot handle him, he is not hopeless. Most aggressive dogs can be brought under control by the proper methods, that being the use of this book or the services of a professional trainer.

Equipment

The equipment used for obedience training is very simple but very important (Illus. 21 and 22). Do not skimp on the proper equipment by trying to make do with what you already have. The correct collar and leash will probably cost you less than the price of this book. If they aren't worth the investment, you shouldn't be training your dog.

A metal chain collar, as shown in Illus. 22, will be needed; this chain collar has two rings, one at each end. The collars come in various lengths from 8 to 32 inches, in two-inch progressions, and in some five different weights of links advancing in thickness from very fine to extra heavy as the length is increased. Try to buy the thickest collar for your particular size of dog; there will

be added strength and much less chance of breakage. Fine or thin chains tend to cut a dog's neck.

Place the chain around your dog's neck by slipping one ring through the other and forming a loop like the letter P with the chain. With your dog facing you, slip the P-shaped loop over his head. When worn correctly (Illus. 23), with the dog on your left side, the collar will release immediately after tightening (Illus. 24). But when put on backwards (Illus. 25 and 26), it will tighten and not release, staying choking tight all the time.

To determine the correct size of chain for your dog, place it around his neck. There should be two inches of overhang (Illus. 27). More than this could cause him to slip out of the collar when you walk him, and less than this would make the collar fit too tightly when it is put over his ears. You would also have too little slack to tighten effectively for corrections. The chain collar can be worn all the time, so long as it fits correctly or snugly.

As for what not to use, do not try to work with a strap collar. This has a fixed size once it is on the dog and offers no correction features. Strap collars are good if you must occasionally tie up your dog. The very thick strap collars are used in guard work. For both of these purposes, the fact that the collar does not tighten can be used to your advantage.

You may be thinking of sparing your dog excess punishment by using a strap collar for obedience training instead of a chain collar. This book is written with the thought of inflicting as little punishment as possible. This is why training with a chain collar is preferred. The chain collar corrects quickly and effectively, encouraging no further resistance. The strap collar will produce little or no correction, but only a nagging pull that encourages resistance and actually continues corrections indefinitely. Precise, effective corrections are necessary to train a dog; these corrections render the strap collar ineffective. Therefore, the wisest and most effective choice is the chain collar.

Another type of collar is called a show choke, which is a fancy version of the choke chain. It tightens only partially and is ineffective for obedience work. There is also a variation of the choke collar called a fur saver. This is a choke chain made of rectangular links. It may save the fur at the cost of the dog's learning. You cannot get effective corrections with it. Some of the fur will fly in training, but this is only temporary and needn't cause any alarm.

A desirable type of collar that you will be able to use later on is called the nylon choke collar. It looks just like the metal choke chain, except that it is made of nylon fabric. This collar will not chop up fur as much as the metal collar will, and it can be used after your dog is well established in his obedience patterns. Part of the effectiveness of the metal chain collar lies in its ability to make noise as well as to provide more stringent corrections than the nylon collar. That is why you should not use the nylon choke collar until your dog works well for you on the metal collar. The chain collars also release after each tightening; the nylon choke leads do not release and have to be manually opened.

We would like to comment about spike or prong collars that are sold indiscriminately by pet shops to people whose big dogs pull them down the street. A spike collar, contrary to popular belief, does not dig into the dog's neck. It corrects by pinching the skin when the prongs come together. Jerking on the collar makes the prongs tighten. This causes about three times the punishment of the chain-collar correction. Casual use of the spike collar can cause irreparable damage to your dog. The spike collar may be used in extreme cases by a professional trainer, but should never be used by any person on his own dog.

The proper training leash should be a six-foot canvas web or leather lead with a bolt snap on one end and a securely finished loop on the other end. The leather leash is the most durable, but also the most costly. Do not buy those brightly colored plastic leashes of various short lengths; they are useless for training purposes. An equally worthless bit of equipment is the metal chain leash. Corrections made with this leash will hurt your hands more than your dog.

Some suppliers make it very hard for you to train your dog by not having the proper equipment in stock. Don't expect to find it in your local supermarket. You will eventually find it in a well-equipped pet shop. A leash with a six-foot length is absolutely necessary to provide an average proper distance between you and your dog on stays. It also allows the proper amount of slack to catch him on right-about turns. There are 10- to 50-foot tracking leads and leashes available, but these have very specific applications and are not used for obedience training.

Obedience Training Schedule

Note: The best way to use this information is to first read the training procedure as applied to the normal/average dog. Then, if your dog falls into one of the six other personality categories, refer to the methods outlined thereafter for your particular type of dog.

First "Week": Getting Your Dog's Attention (Illus. 28–33)

DAY ONE
The Normal/Average Dog
Begin the first day's training session by attaching the six-foot web training leash to your dog's collar and putting the choke chain around your dog's neck in the correct fashion: Make the letter P with the chain and slip it over his head with him facing you. The dog is now attired for serious training sessions.

Your dog can be on either side of you. Put your right-hand thumb through the end loop of the leash. Close your fist on the leash. Clasp your left hand over your right hand (Illus. 28). You are holding the leash at its end and the entire six-foot length is between you and your dog. Then, without saying a word to your dog, just start walking. This can be in the backyard, in front of your house, or on a quiet street nearby, just as long as there are not too many distractions. Don't ask his permission, don't beg him, don't say HEEL because he is not heeling yet. Just walk. Walk at a normal place from one end of your yard to another, and stop. Once you get there, just relax for about 20 seconds. Look around, ignoring your dog; don't look at him. Then, suddenly, without any warning, start walking back to the other side and continue until you get there.

Your dog may lie down and/or howl. You have never done this to him before. You have always coaxed and humored him, followed the dictates of his desires, but now you are walking and he is probably being dragged, possibly walking, jumping on you, or even attempting to nip you. He might be running in front of you so that you actually fall over him. He could be trying anything to prevent your getting from one point to the other without having his permission or approval.

Whatever your pet's ploy, you must continue until you reach your objective, the starting point. Once you get there, take another break of maybe half a minute and then start back to the far side again. Continue walking at a normal pace even if your dog lunges in front of you, away from you, or howls in frantic indignation. No matter what he does, ignore him. Don't look at him; just continue to walk at a normal pace. If he tangles the leash by stepping on it, let it remain that way. Just drag him across the yard. Once you get to your stopping point, take a half-minute pause, again ignoring your dog. Then start again, walking back to the other point. Continue this for about 15 minutes; then give your dog a break.

For the break you need a 20-foot clothesline with a bolt snap attached at one end, which makes for quick and easy installation and removal (Illus. 29). When you are ready to give your dog his break, first snap on the clothesline, and then remove the leash. You should be holding the end of the 20-foot clothesline looped around your thumb. Take off the leash, toss it on the ground in front of your dog, and, in a loud, happy voice, tell him OKAY, THAT'S ALL.

Illus. 15. The sit-stay command with the puppy on the full six feet of leash.

Illus. 16. The stay correction.

Illus. 18. Renewing the stay command from six feet away.

Illus. 17. The new stay command.

Depending on what category your dog is in, there will be different reactions to this release. What you do is more important than what he does. Your dog's reactions may range from taking off at full speed like a rocket to just standing near you. Looking at you. If he takes off like a rocket, silently turn in the opposite direction, gripping the line tightly with both hands, and run, with equal thrust and speed, away from the dog. When your dog runs out of line, this will cause a terrific impact as he is jerked back forcefully towards you. You should not yell anything at him or communicate verbally with him in any way (Illus. 30). All you should do, immediately after the impact, is walk towards your dog. Walking towards him puts back the necessary slack in the clothesline that will be needed for his next charge.

Your dog will probably get up and look at you in a very puzzled way, trying to figure out what happened because this has never occurred before. He will probably make another charge as determined as the first. Let him take off and, once again, you should turn and run hard in the opposite direction, producing the same silent, powerful correction.

After two of these corrections, a lot of dogs are convinced that this rocketlike charge is definitely not a good thing to do. For a few more determined dogs, it may take four, five, or more corrections before the same results are achieved. Your dog is learning that something bad will happen to him if he tries to run away from you. He may learn not to run away after one correction, or after ten corrections, but learn he will if you do your part correctly. Make as many corrections as are needed to produce the desired response. The ideal response is that your dog will stand near you, looking at you, showing little or no desire to run away (Illus. 31). This response is usually achieved in two corrections with most dogs.

During the break you should also not speak to your dog. There should be no praise after the correction and no praise when the dog watches and stays close to you. The dog is not reacting to please you; he is just finding out what is safest and most comfortable for him. Lessons learned in this way will be long-lasting.

The above procedures may be frowned upon by some well-meaning, but misguided people. Although these people are critical about what they consider to be your cruel training methods, and will voice their objections, they have no compunction about having a dog destroyed or given away because of housebreaking, chewing, or obedience problems. If these people make remarks about the way you are handling your dog, ignore them.

After about a five-minute break, swap the clothesline for the leash and repeat exactly the same noncommunicative walking you did before. This should last another

15 minutes, again followed by a five-minute break, as outlined previously, which will end the session for the first day.

The Overfriendly Dog, the High-Strung Dog, and the Aloof Dog

For all of these dogs, you should follow the same procedure as you used for the normal/average dog.

The Shy/Fearful Dog

Sometimes, in extreme cases, the shy/fearful dog should be verbally praised for walking. This provides an incentive for him to continue walking and diminishes the need for unpleasant dragging, which is not beneficial to this particular type of dog. If, however, he must be dragged, shorter distances usually work better.

The Fearful Biter

The fearful biter will not normally bite you during the attention-getter. If he does make an all-out attack, this may indicate that you have incorrectly classified an aggressive dog as a fearful biter. If such is the case, then go on to the instructions for the aggressive dog.

In rare instances, the fearful biter may try to bite you. Since he prefers attacking from behind, the attention-getter, with its full six feet of leash, provides him with the opportunity to go behind you, bite, and run a safe six feet away. This differs from an aggressive dog's all-out frontal attack. Biting from behind and then running away indicates that you have correctly classified your dog as a fearful biter.

To handle the problem of a fearful biter biting you from behind, you must limit the freedom of movement that the dog will have on the leash and restrict his opportunity to move behind you and get away from you. This is done by completely bypassing the attention-getter and going right on to heeling, as described in the next section, which will bring the dog in very close proximity to you. Your dog should be walking on about two feet of leash, and thus he will be unable to get behind you for a bite and then run a safe six feet away.

If you have the type of fearful bitter who will bite other people but not you, or who just chooses not to bite you, then you can continue with the attention-getter as described above with the five-minute breaks after each 15-minute training session.

The Aggressive Dog

The aggressive dog may not like running to the end of the leash and being jerked, with the attendant surprise and discomfort that this correction causes. He may possibly turn around and bite you. With the aggressive dog,

44

it is important that he be praised verbally, immediately after a correction.

If the aggressive dog runs around and barks or growls or both, continue to walk. Regardless of how obstinate he becomes, continue to walk until you have reached your predetermined stopping point. If he is running alongside of you, jumping and mounting or even nipping lightly, do not allow him to deter you. He fully expects that his actions will deter you, and you must prove him wrong. Try to keep your hands away from him. Continue walking, clasping both hands together and touching your chest. This position serves best to absorb impacts. It also presents the least threatening posture to your dog and leaves him no protrusive objects to grab onto and bite.

Nothing short of an all-out biting attack should stop you from walking. If your dog's bullying tactics are unsuccessful, they will diminish and he will stop. As this occurs, he will slowly change his attitude and will gain new respect for you, making it possible to work him and make him a valuable member of the household.

If you are able to work your aggressive dog, you should work him as described previously, with two 15-minute sessions and the controlled five-minute breaks after each session. If, however, your dog actually bites you, you have a serious problem requiring the help of a professional trainer. When a dog will bite you for almost no reason at all, neither one of you will last through the more rigid requirements that are part of the rest of the obedience training. A professional dog trainer should be called immediately.

THE SECOND DAY

The Normal/Average Dog
The second day's training consists of an exact repetition of the first day's procedure. As you start to walk, you may be pleasantly surprised by your dog's change in attitude. You may find that, as you continue to walk without saying a word to your dog, he is moving at your side. Continue the same routine for the second day: 15 minutes and a five-minute break; then 15 more minutes, a final five-minute break; then stop for the day. Make sure your dog hasn't eaten anything for at least one and a half hours prior to each training session.

After each training session, ignore your dog for about 15 minutes. Don't sympathize with him, play with him, or let anyone else heap condolences upon him, affirming in his mind what a bad, abusive time he had. Keep everyone away from him. Let him be alone to think over what has just happened. As in the first day's procedure,

your two 15-minute training sessions should each be followed by the same five-minute breaks on the long clothesline. By the end of the second day, your dog should be increasingly attentive. Every time you start to walk, he should be moving along with you.

The Overfriendly Dog and the High-Strung Dog
These dogs should be calming down as they are being worked into each consecutive day.

The Aloof Dog
The aloof dog may still be resisting you by holding back. He must be dragged and not allowed to bring a halt to the training session by not walking. He must learn that this tactic will avail him nothing. Continue to drag him, possibly even running, and he will soon choose to walk. You must outlast him and be more stubborn than he is.

The Shy/Fearful Dog, the Fearful Biter, and the Aggressive Dog
These dogs should be more secure and confident as days go by. Continue the regular routine as their confidence grows.

THE THIRD DAY

All Dogs
Follow the same procedures as for the second day with all of these dogs.

THE FOURTH DAY

All Dogs
Follow the same procedures as for the second and third days with all of these dogs. By the end of the fourth day's training, your dog (no matter what his category) should be walking when you walk, stopping when you stop, and paying more attention to you than you ever thought was possible (Illus. 32).

THE FIFTH DAY

The Normal/Average Dog
We will begin the fifth day's training lesson with the 20-foot-long clothesline that was previously used on the breaks. Discard the six-foot leash for now; you are ready for what we will call Attention Motivation. This will be in the form of a distraction and correction.

The best distractions are the things your dog likes best or goes for most enthusiastically. This could be another dog, a favorite human playmate, children walking, a cat crossing his path, or any other irresistible force that will

Illus. 19. Returning slowly from the full six-foot distance.

Illus. 20. Praising the puppy with the words GOOD BOY on your return from the stay command.

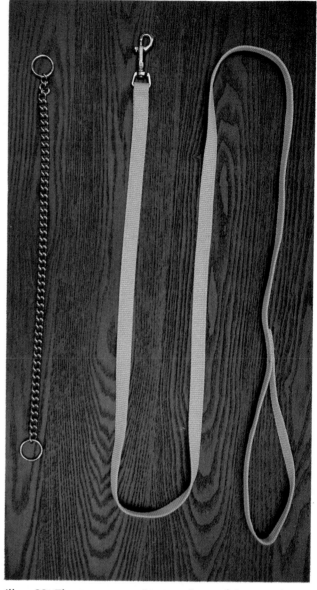

Illus. 22. The proper equipment for training your dog consists of a metal chain collar and a six-foot leather- or canvas-web or nylon leash.

Illus. 21. Shown here are examples of nylon choke collars, which can be used on small breeds of dogs and dogs with sensitive skin, and strap collars, on which to place identification tags.

47

make your dog forget about you and charge towards the distraction.

In order to be effective, the distraction must be a completely controllable situation. This means that both the distraction and the environment must be controlled. A fenced-in backyard or an isolated park or beach area is preferable to the streets of a heavily trafficked city where all kinds of enticements can suddenly appear that will make contact with your dog and nullify the effectiveness of this lesson.

The dog or cat distraction must be held on a leash or tied to a fence or post and not be allowed to make contact with your dog. Children can be enlisted to help you by walking or running past your dog, but they must follow your instructions closely and not be allowed to touch or pet the dog while they are being used as the distraction. At this time, no distraction should be allowed closer than ten feet from your dog, both during the training session and during the following break.

You should begin training by gripping the end of the line tightly. As your dog breaks and runs towards the distraction, you should silently turn and run in the opposite direction. There will be a powerful impact as your dog reaches the end of the line which will be made even more forceful by your running. Your dog may stand motionless, watching you, after this first correction. If he does, you should still ignore him and continue your walking routine, being always watchful for another charge towards the distraction. (The distraction should remain present during the entire training session, but remove it on the break.)

Let us assume that your dog does not learn on the first correction, but makes a second lunge at the distraction. He may make this second try immediately after the first, or he may let time elapse before trying again. In either case, your reaction should be the same. Silently make a turnabout, while tightly clutching the end loop of the line to your chest, and forcefully run in the opposite direction, away from your dog. After the impact, you should take about four steps towards your dog, creating a slack in the line that is necessary for a further correction should he make another attempt.

If more attempts are made, your reaction will remain the same—say nothing. You should continue to correct your dog until the desired result is achieved—that result being that your dog watches you instead of the distraction at hand. It does not matter if your dog is barking, whining, or otherwise making any kind of oral protest. Any of this is permissible as long as he is watching you and not charging the distraction. Ignore any oral protestation your dog makes. Only correct him for running towards the distraction.

In case your conscience is bothering you about the severity of these corrections, or in case you have a couple of so-called "experts" advising you that this is no way to treat a dog, remember that there is a very important reason for the severity of the corrections: You are teaching your dog that he must not run away from you after cats or dogs or any other distraction. This conditioning will be his life-insurance policy. If he chases a cat across the street into traffic, he will be killed. If you fail to correct hard now, someday a car or truck will do the job for you, and it will not be the least bit gentle. We have never seen or heard of one dog, of the hundreds of dogs we train each year, being hurt in any way by this method of correction.

By the end of the first 15-minute session on this fifth day, your dog should be walking along fairly close to you, looking around but ignoring the distraction that took complete command of his attention in the beginning of the lesson (Illus. 33).

This session will be followed by the usual five-minute break without the distraction present. The break is on the same 20-foot line that was just used in the training session.

After the break, start the second session, which is an exact repetition of the first. Bring the distraction in again. Most dogs will ignore it, but should your dog charge, make sure you react with an equal charge of your own. This, followed by a five-minute break with the distraction removed, will end the fifth day's training session for the normal/average dog. Leave your dog alone for about 15 minutes, giving him a chance to think over what has just happened to him. If you do your part well, he should have a lot to think about.

The Overfriendly Dog and the High-Strung Dog
These two dogs will provide plenty of action for you with repeated lunges at distractions. They may bark a lot and should be ignored completely; they're not easily discouraged from their favorite pursuits. Once again, you cannot allow their boundless energy and enthusiasm to defeat you. Your determination and calm persistence will eventually override the dog's most insistent attempts to disregard you. If you feel at odds with the world or short-tempered, do not allow this feeling to influence your behavior with the dog. He will sense it and use your weakness to his advantage.

Each time the dog lunges for the distraction, silently clasp your hands to your chest with a firm grip on the line and run in the opposite direction. After the impact, put slack in the line by taking a few steps towards your dog. When he finally decides not to try any more charges towards the distraction, just turn and walk away towards the other stopping point. Walk back again towards the distraction, and if your dog tries to run to the distraction, simply repeat the process once more. After a while, your dog will choose to watch you rather than the distraction. The same training format should apply, consisting of two sessions in distractions followed by the usual two five-minute breaks. This will end the fifth day's lesson.

The Aloof Dog and the Shy/Fearful Dog

These two types may only take one or two steps towards the distraction. It may take a while for them to build up their confidence to charge for a distraction. Some of them may not. Whatever your dog's choice, continue to avail him of every opportunity to pursue the distractions and receive the attendant correction. Give him the usual two sessions, followed by the two five-minute breaks.

You may have to increase the distractions for these dogs. It is reasonable to increase them to a maximum in this situation by having a neighbor call and coax your dog over to him, but it would be unfair to have a member of your own immediate family call him directly.

These dogs will appear to have learned with very few corrections, possibly even only one. Though it appears over, do not be fooled.

The Fearful Biter and the Aggressive Dog

These dogs will run directly for the distraction, giving you plenty of action, but they should respond quickly to very few corrections. It is possible that, after one of these corrections, the fearful biter or the aggressive dog may turn on you and try to bite you. With both of these dogs, *immediately after the correction give them verbal praise* and continue walking away as before. The praise will serve to turn aside any immediate thoughts your dog may have of biting you. A few split seconds of reassurance could make the difference between a mistake on his part and a victory for you. Even if your dog comes at you growling, you must praise him. Nothing short of an all-out biting attack should deter you. The fact that he was upset enough almost to bite you indicates that he will be too upset to invite many more of these disturbing corrections. The usual walking back and forth, with the five-minute breaks, will end this routine.

THE SIXTH DAY

The Normal/Average Dog

On the sixth day again use distractions. They should be the most extreme distractions available around your home, but bear in mind that, although most distractions will be ignored by your dog, there are some few distrac-

tions that are unfair to expect your dog to ignore at this level of his training. An example of an unfair tactic would be if the cat or dog being used as a distraction made physical contact with your dog or if a member of your immediate family were to call your dog by name to come to him. At this stage of your dog's training, it would not be fair to expect him to ignore such distractions.

On the other hand, examples of fair distractions that your dog must ignore are a neighbor or someone not in the immediate family calling your dog by name to come to him or a member of the immediate family yelling, clapping, running, or otherwise calling attention to himself, so long as he doesn't directly call the dog to him.

When using distractions on your dog, use fair distractions for the present. As we near the end of the course of training, your dog should listen to you against any distraction, be it fair or unfair.

You should start the sixth day's training with multiple distractions readied in your area. Once again, start walking from point to point. You can have cats and dogs staked out in different areas of your yard. Have children and adults run around and call your dog. People could be whistling or banging pots and pans. Whistling and snapping fingers is a fair distraction no matter who does it, but whistling and snapping fingers must never be used by you to call your dog to you.

This day's session will once again consist of the usual two 15-minute work sessions in distractions and the usual five-minute break after each without the distractions. This could mean walking your dog to the front of the house if distractions have been staked out in the backyard. While on the break, if your dog should go for one of the distractions you have set, respond by implementing the usual severe correction. Make an abrupt turnabout and run forcefully the other way before you run out of line. Remember, you need a certain amount of slack in the line to effect the desired correction.

Your actions will make the critical difference between real obedience that works anywhere and anytime and the fake obedience that only works in certain situations. Your dog is learning by being corrected while on his break that he must always ignore distractions, with or without your direct attention. This attitude should make all subsequent training commands extremely effective and reliable.

The Overfriendly Dog and the High-Strung Dog

These dogs should be handled in the same way as the normal/average dog and should be responding excellently. They should be calmed to a great degree by the training.

Illus. 23. Correct collar installation consists of installing the collar shaped like the letter P with the dog facing you.

Illus. 24. A side view of the correct collar installation.

Illus. 25. Here the collar is being installed backwards.

Illus. 26. A side view of the wrong way to install the collar. It is being installed backwards.

The Aloof Dog

The aloof dog still may not be walking freely by himself. You may have to drag him, and drag him you should. He may have decided that he does not like the training and, by refusing to walk, thinks he can put a halt to it. You must make doubly sure that he is not successful in his attempt to stop you. Not only is it correct for you to walk and drag him, it is even better if you can run and drag him. He will eventually give in and walk. He is hoping that you will weaken and give up before he does. If he is successful now, then he has halted your training, proving that he is the master. However, if you win out, you begin a permanent, positive change in his attitude that will ensure your success with the rest of the training. Under no circumstances should the aloof dog be coaxed into walking. He should be dragged as you walk or run silently. He must be made to walk because he is commanded to, not because someone is coaxing him.

The Shy/Fearful Dog

The shy/fearful dog should be treated the same as the normal/average dog with the exception that he will be verbally praised with the words GOOD BOY every time he requires a correction. When he overcomes his fear of walking with you, he can be praised just for walking. Take note that the shy/fearful dog is trained with almost a completely opposite technique to the aloof dog, showing, once again, the absolute necessity to categorize your dog correctly from the beginning.

The Fearful Biter

On this sixth day the fearful biter is treated exactly as the normal/average dog. Ignore him completely as you walk.

The Aggressive Dog

The aggressive dog is treated exactly the same as the normal/average dog with the exception that you verbally praise him immediately following any necessary corrections. Give him the usual two sessions and two subsequent breaks.

THE SEVENTH DAY

All Dogs

All these dogs are worked identically, in the same fashion as was the normal/average dog on the sixth day. There should be no verbal communication and no coaxing or praising. This will bring all the different types of dogs as close to the response of the normal/average dog as is possible, by conditioning them for one entire day with no special concessions as were previously needed for each specific type of dog. You should now have a dog who walks when you walk, stops when you stop, stays reasonably close to you, and watches you no matter what the distraction—all this without your giving any commands or communicating in any manner whatsoever. The seventh day consists of the same two 15-minute sessions, followed by the usual five-minute breaks.

THE EIGHTH DAY

All Dogs

The eighth day of training consists of a test for your dog; you must plan carefully so that everything is done exactly right for the test. Remove all distractions from your training area. Have your helper ready to assist you by displaying your dog's favorite distractions. This could be a cat held in his arms, a dog on a leash, a broom, or two pot covers that are clanged together, etc.

You should enter the training area with your dog on the 20-foot clothesline and begin walking across the area towards the opposite side. As you get halfway across the area, your helper should pop out from a predetermined hiding place, holding the distraction or bringing it with him. He should move out into your clear view with the distraction and remain there.

After the distraction is visible for three seconds, you should silently turn and walk rapidly away from it. If your dog comes with you before the line tightens to jerk or pull him, then he has passed the test. If your dog hesitates and requires a tug before he comes away with you, then he needs further testing. If your dog walks or lunges towards the distraction, he has failed the test and should be corrected in the usual manner by your turning and running away in the opposite direction.

If your dog has failed the test, making a correction necessary, then you must continue for another two days with heavy distractions before you can again attempt to test your dog. If your dog stands looking at the distraction, but does not charge it, then you almost have his complete attention. Work him for another five minutes with no distraction, and then have your helper reappear abruptly with the distraction. If your dog comes around with you, he has passed the test. If he still shows interest in the distraction, work him for another two days in heavy distraction, and then test him once more.

For those dogs who pass the test the first time, no further work is needed. Whether your dog passes the test the first time or you have to use heavy distractions for two more days or however long it takes, he must pass the test before you can go on. Once your dog successfully passes the test, you are to be congratulated, for you have done something that even some so-called professional dog trainers are not capable of doing or don't know how to do. You now have your dog's complete attention. Now you can begin heeling on the leash.

The Second "Week": Heeling
(Illus. 34–49)

THE FIRST DAY
The Normal/Average Dog

This training lesson will again consist of two 15-minute work sessions followed by the usual five-minute breaks. The training area should be the same as used for the attention-getter. You should again be using your 20-foot clothesline for the breaks; it should be lying on the ground in your working area so that it can be quickly and easily installed for the breaks.

Begin with your dog on the six-foot leash. Your right-hand thumb should be placed through the end loop of the leash and your hand closed upon it. With your left hand, grab the middle of the leash and again place this middle part over your right thumb. Open and close your right hand, grabbing the entire leash. Now, your left hand grabs the entire leash just below and touching your right hand. As you lift up your hands and look at them in front of you, they should be in the same basic position as if you were holding a basketball bat. Remember, both hands must be together and touching each other. Study Illus. 34–36, so that you can grip the leash correctly.

You can practise this grip without your dog. Just snap the leash onto a fence or banister to enable you to practise till you are confident and can assume the proper grip quickly. This preparation is very important, so that you do not fumble in front of your dog and allow him to think you are not confident and in complete control.

Up to this point, we have allowed your dog to walk on either side of you. We now need him on the left side only (Illus. 37). This is accomplished by grabbing the leash with both hands in the proper way and rotating your body clockwise until your dog ends up on your left side. From now on, no matter where your dog's position, anytime you wish to begin heeling him you should spin your body in a clockwise circle that will cause your dog to wind up on your left. Once he is on your left side, you are immediately ready to begin heeling.

The heeling command consists of two words spoken in a normal, level tone of voice. It should not sound as if you are begging, nor should it sound loud and frightening. The first word is your dog's name, immediately followed by the command word HEEL. It would sound like this: JOE, HEEL. As the command is spoken, you must simultaneously begin walking, taking off on your left foot. Never give the HEEL command standing motionless, expecting your dog will walk. He won't. Just give the command, JOE, HEEL, and begin walking across your training area.

The preliminary work on the long clothesline should

eliminate any mad charges by your dog. However, as you walk across the training area, you will probably find your dog leading slightly out in front of you. Your reaction to his pulling or wandering out in front of you should be a quick, silent, surprise right about-turn with a simultaneous rearward jerk on the leash as you turn and walk rapidly in the opposite direction. The next time that your dog gets out in front of you, again use the same surprising right about-turn. This turn should be used as the correction for your dog every time he gets out in front of you.

The right about-turn should be made in one quick, sharp movement and not in a slow circle. The surprise and shock of a complete 180-degree turnabout correction delivered every time he gets out in front of you, and the lack of it when he stays by your side, will soon convince your dog that it is much more comfortable to be by your side—more comfortable than out in front of you where he can't watch you and where you may be able to catch him with your sneaky right about-turns.

After a few of these hard right about-turn corrections, you may find your dog overacting slightly by hanging back, so that you are pulling him along. This is perfectly normal, and even good. It shows you that he is trying his best. He doesn't like the corrections and has decided to stay back where he can watch you safely. Your response to this should be not to coax him but to speed up the turns.

It is important to correct him as he starts lagging, pulling out in front, or doing anything other than heeling at your side (Illus 38–40). It will be easier for him to learn what he should be doing if he is corrected while making the mistake rather than after the fact. A great means of building your dog's confidence is praising him. The opportunity for praise occurs when you stop. Your dog should stop by your side, still standing, paying attention to you. You should praise him by stroking his head and telling him, GOOD BOY, VERY GOOD.

It should be mentioned that some dogs will naturally sit upon stopping, even before having been taught the formal sit command. This, too, is perfectly fine, and you should praise your dog for whatever he does naturally, be it sit or stand. At this stage, your dog is being praised for stopping at your side when you stop, not for doing an automatic sit, which will come later on in training. Some dogs will joyfully show their anticipation of this praise by wagging their tails just before being praised. This is a very good sign.

You should be walking back and forth, making right about-turns and running, where necessary, to correct lagging. Intermittently stop and praise your dog as described above. He may dislike the training, but he will

Illus. 27. Allow a two-inch overhang, for proper fit.

Illus. 28. The attention getter.

54

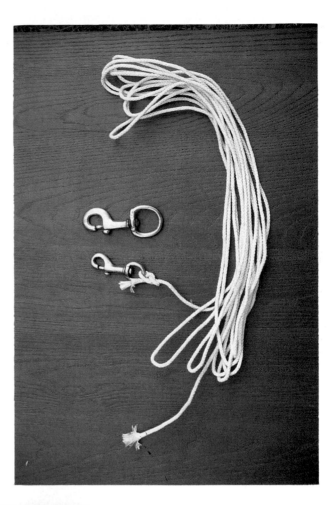

Illus. 29. Use a cotton clothesline and bolt-snap equipment for long line work.

Illus. 30. Making a correction on the clothesline.

love the praise. Pat him on the head rather than scratching his chest or rubbing his belly. You want to show him that his actions please you, not that you are playing a game with him.

After 15 minutes of this exercise, you should walk near the area where you have laid down the long clothesline. With one smooth motion, quickly attach the bolt snap of the clothesline to his collar. Still holding his leash in your hand, reach down, unhook the leash, and toss it on the ground about four feet in front of your dog, telling him in a level but cheerful voice, OKAY, THAT'S ALL. Any attempt at mad charges by your dog after receiving this release should be met by the usual clothesline corrections, with you running the opposite way. Your dog should, after his previous conditioning, take his break with the clothesline dragging, staying relatively close to you and keeping a watchful eye on you.

After the usual five-minute-break, reinstall the leash. Take off the line and let it lie on the ground. Continue with an exact repetition of the first 15-minute session, correcting your dog for running out in front of you and for lagging. This should again be followed by a break, in the same manner, as before. This will end the first day's training session for the normal dog.

The Overfriendly Dog and the High-Strung Dog

These dogs are wilder than most, and may try to take advantage of you and the change in equipment by leading out in front. They should be corrected in the same basic way, with a right about-turn, with the exception that the correction must be made more intensely. Begin heeling by holding the leash as described previously. Release the lower grip you have with your right hand. The technique that follows should be practiced without your dog on the leash until you become proficient at it.

Holding the leash with your right hand only, as your dog runs out in front of you, open your right hand and release the entire six-foot body of the leash, but keep your right-hand thumb through the end loop (Illus. 41). Close your fist around the entire end loop, holding it very securely, thereby bracing for a very severe correction. As the slack is being released, make a quick right about-turn and begin walking rapidly in the opposite direction (Illus. 42). In this way, the impact of the right about-turn correction is intensified by the time provided while you and your dog are moving away from each other rapidly, before the slack is taken up, causing a terrific impact (Illus. 43). These turns should be made as long as your dog continues to go out in front of you. Your left hand will not be needed at all in this routine and should only be used after the turn to place the slack of the leash back into your right hand.

In all other ways, these dogs should be treated as the normal/average dogs; this includes your running whenever they tend to lag. As the severity of his charge diminishes, he should be treated exactly as the normal/average dog, which includes the two-handed grip on the leash as the right about-turns are made in the normal way.

The reason that the right about-turn is made without yelling NO and without any communication between you and your dog is simple and basic: You are trying, by your actions, to gain the attention of the dog. If you tell him NO or communicate with or warn him in any other way that you are about to make a right about-turn, then the effectiveness of the correction is lost. The suddenness of the correction and the discomfort produced by it are what make it effective. If your dog does not know when you are going to make your about-turn correction, and if you don't cue him by telling him NO, then your dog is forced to watch you, which is exactly what we want.

Another reason for making the about-turn with a silent correction is that you want the dog to think that he and his lack of attention caused the correction, and not that you decided to jerk him all of a sudden. Dogs that are trained with this silent method of correction behave in a superior manner to other dogs that are trained by both vocal and physical corrections. This is true even when the latter group of dogs are trained, or even owned, by professional trainers. These dogs may behave obediently but do not keep a watchful eye on their masters, and so cannot be worked on the leash as well.

Both overfriendly dogs and high-strung dogs should be praised verbally only. The praise should be a quick GOOD BOY, and then you should immediately move on to a new HEEL command. This is done to discourage the dog from misconstruing your praise as a release from training. Work your right about-turns and stops abruptly, every couple of yards. As you stop, with your dog standing, praise him verbally with the words GOOD BOY, and then quickly say JOE, HEEL, and walk off another couple of yards. Stop again and repeat the praise. Two 15-minute sessions of heeling and praising, plus the five-minute breaks on the long line, will end the lesson for the first day.

The Aloof Dog

The aloof dog will not try running out in front of you with much force and should be handled with the two-handed leash grip. When training him, you will have to run and drag him more than you will have to make right about-turn corrections.

The aloof dog is one of the very few classifications of dogs that can be considered stubborn. It could take days of dragging to get him to walk freely by your side; in some rare instances it could take weeks. You must be more persistent than your dog and outlast him. Never let this dog get you angry with his refusal to walk. Just continue breaking into runs and show him he will be much more comfortable staying up and walking by your side. You must only break into a run when he is holding back, never when he is at your side. He will eventually come to believe that his lagging is the very thing that causes your running and the accompanying dragging correction. He will finally decide that the safest place to be is at your side. But let him make this decision by himself; don't try to nag or coax him into it.

The aloof dog should be praised on the stops just as the normal/average dog. This should be both physical and verbal praise as you stop walking and your dog remains standing. Continue your heeling routine for two 15-minute sessions, running where necessary to correct his hanging back, and making your definitive stops, praising him immediately as you stop.

The aloof dog may try to sit, pulling back as you stop. Keep the leash very short so he won't be able to do this. Continue to grip the leash, providing tension and discomfort so long as he continues pulling back on the leash. Under no circumstances should you walk back to where your dog indicates his preferred position to be and praise him there. You are undoing your victories on the heeling by allowing him to win on the stops. Move right on to a new HEEL command, and continue with the routine of heeling with intermittent stops for the two 15-minute sessions and the controlled five-minute breaks on the long line after each.

The Shy/Fearful Dog

The shy/fearful dog should respond very well and very quickly to the right about-turn corrections as used with the normal/average dog. (This means both hands are holding the leash in the normal way.) He may, after only one or two corrections, be hanging back to avoid any more corrections. Deal with this behavior in the usual manner—by running.

This dog should be treated in the same manner as the normal/average dog, with the exception that he should be praised verbally for walking at your side. In fact, heavily praise the shy/fearful dog, both verbally and physically, to build up his confidence. This should be done as soon as possible after stopping, to avoid increased fear and apprehension on his part. The shy/fearful dog may try to sit or even lie down from fear. If he sits, this is okay. Just praise him and then go on to a new HEEL command. However, if he succeeds in lying down, lift him up into the sit position by putting your left hand inside his collar on top. Lift him straight up into the sit position while praising him, thereby somewhat reducing his apprehension.

The best approach is to avoid letting your dog lie down. This can be accomplished by praising him, immediately upon stopping, not giving the dog a chance to lie down, and then immediately moving on to a new HEEL command. Should your dog begin to lie down in spite of your praises, give instantaneously a new HEEL command and being to walk, making it impossible for him to lie down. Work your dog on heeling for two 15-minute sessions, followed by two five-minute breaks on the long line.

The Fearful Biter (A)

The information that follows pertains to the dog who *could not* be worked on the previous attention-getter because he would have bitten you if you worked on the long clothesline. Since he has proven he will bite, certain safety precautions should be taken. The necessary equipment consists of a sturdy metal or wooden stake and 12 feet of clothesline with a bolt snap on one end. The best kind of stake is the one resembling a corkscrew that is sold in pet shops and is used to tie up a dog outdoors. You will also need another chain collar, which should be bigger, stronger, and heavier than your dog's regular collar.

In the center of your training area, install the stake, making sure it is very securely embedded. Attach one end of the 12-foot clothesline to the stake; then, to the other end of the clothesline attach the bolt snap with the heavy chain collar. Leave the collar laid out on the ground, already hooked to the line and ready to be slipped over your dog's head.

Bring your dog into the area on a leash. Walk directly to the collar and slip it over his head; it doesn't matter if the collar is put on frontwards or rearwards. Gripping the leash in the proper way, as described for the normal/average dog, begin walking in a counterclockwise circle around the stake, with your dog at your left side. There can be no right about-turns so long as your dog is hooked to this safety clotheslines, but your dog also cannot bite you. For, if he tried, you have only to step back out of the 12-foot circle and he will be stopped completely by the 12-foot safety line.

If your dog decides he does not like this routine of walking with you and, in fact, tries to bite you, you cannot work him further and must consult a professional trainer.

The purpose of this training is to teach your dog that he cannot successfully bite you and that he is better off walking with you and not trying to bite. The first day's training will consist of one ten-minute session and will end up with you removing the leash and leaving the dog tied to the stake to think over what has happened, with

Illus. 31. The dog standing attentively on the clothes-line.

Illus. 32. The dog coming around on the long line without a correction.

Illus. 33. The dog coming around, ignoring the distraction.

Illus. 34–36. Taking up the leash.

Illus. 35.

Illus. 36.

you remaining in the area. After the break, reinstall the leash and take the dog out of the training area. This will end the first day's lesson in heeling.

The fearful biter should receive verbal praise only on all the stops; keep your hand firmly gripping the leash. There are no right about-turns as yet, so just continue heeling in a counterclockwise direction, stopping every few yards to verbally praise your dog with the words GOOD BOY. Repeat this for the entire ten-minute session. Your dog should receive his five-minute break on the safety line as described above; then end the training session for this first day of heeling.

The Fearful Biter (B)

The information here pertains to the fearful biter who has been worked on the attention-getter. This dog should be treated exactly as the normal/average dog (with a two-handed leash grip) with the exception that he should be verbally praised immediately after every right about-turn correction. This immediate praise after the corrections helps to thwart any thoughts he may have of biting you. He should also be praised, only verbally, on your stops that will occur every couple of yards. If the dog lags behind, do not correct him by running, as you did for the normal/average dog. Just quicken your pace slightly and keep him close to you. Two 10-minute sessions, each followed by a five-minute break on the long line, will end the first day's session on heeling for this dog.

The Aggressive Dog

Even though your dog is aggressive, it was possible for you to work him on the long line and give him fairly drastic corrections. Therefore, it should be possible to work him on the leash. He also should be worked like the normal/average dog (with a two-handed leash grip) with the exception that he too should be verbally praised immediately following all right about-turn corrections. If the aggressive dog should choose to hang back, you should not break into a run but should only quicken your pace, at the same time giving a new HEEL command.

If the aggressive dog attempts to bite you at this stage of the training, give him two or three days' work around the circular stake and safety line (Illus. 44), as described previously for the fearful biter, and then try again. The safety-line work can give the fearful biter and the aggressive dog the confidence and security that will calm them, and thus enable you to work them. This very often can save the dog's life in cases where the dog would otherwise have to be destroyed or given away because of his aggressiveness or biting problem.

Some dogs may require three or four days on the safety line before they can be worked on the regular heeling routine with right about-turns. Remember, it doesn't matter how long it takes; it matters who wins, you or the dog. In most cases, if you cannot train an aggressive dog, he will eventually die as a result. It is essential that you persist in your efforts until you are successful.

Work your dog on the right about-turns, keeping him close to you and verbally praising with the words GOOD BOY after each correction. Stop every couple of yards and praise your dog for stopping; only verbal praise should be used. Keep a firm two-handed leash grip at all times. Work the usual two 15-minute sessions and follow with the usual two five-minute breaks on the long line. This ends the first day's heeling for the aggressive dog.

THE SECOND DAY

The Normal/Average Dog

Continue with an exact repetition of the first day's training. Your dog's attention should be growing. The workout should consist of the usual two 15-minute sessions, followed by the controlled five-minute breaks after each.

The Overfriendly Dog and the High-Strung Dog

With these dogs repeat the regimen of the first day, with the absence of verbal communication on the corrections. Do two 15-minute sessions, followed by the two five-minute breaks. This will end the session for this second day.

The Aloof Dog, The Shy/Fearful Dog, The Fearful Biter (A and B), and the Aggressive Dog

Each of these dogs should be drilled exactly as he was on the first day of training.

THE THIRD DAY

The Normal/Average Dog

On the third day of training introduce a distraction. It should be posted at one end of the training area, and can be the usual dog or cat or other distraction as used in the attention-getter. Enter the training area from the opposite end, with your dog on the leash, and give the HEEL command. You will be as far away as possible from the distraction, allowing your dog plenty of time to see it.

Walk towards the distraction until you are some ten feet from it. At this point make a hard, sharp, right about-turn; your dog should come around with you. Make this right about-turn with both your hands on the leash in the usual way. If your dog comes around freely on the turn, there should be no accompanying jerk on the leash. If, however, your dog is more occupied with the distraction than with you, your right about-turn should be made with a hard jerk on the leash.

Whether or not your dog needs the correction, turn and walk away from the distraction, and then do another right about-turn and walk towards the distraction again. In the middle of your area you should abruptly stop walking. Your dog should stop and stand, looking at you. At this time, you should praise him physically and verbally. Then give a new HEEL command and take off on your left foot, moving towards the distraction again. Continue walking your dog in the same way, forward and back in a straight line, alternating between about-turns and complete stops, with you praising him. Two sessions of this routine, plus the usual break after each, will end this day's training session for the normal/average dog. The breaks should be made with the distraction removed.

The Overfriendly Dog, the High-Strung Dog, the Aloof Dog, the Shy/Fearful Dog, and the Fearful Biter (B)

These dogs should be worked exactly as the normal/average dog on this third day, with a distraction at one end of the area.

The Fearful Biter (A) and the Aggressive Dog

The fearful biter was worked on the safety line and stake for the first two days. On this third day, he should come off the stake, and both he and the aggressive dog should be worked in the same way. They should not be introduced to any distractions yet. You should heel them, making about-turns with a two-handed leash grip. Make your corrections light on the about-turns and give verbal praise (with the words GOOD BOY) as you make the turns. Stop and praise your dog, verbally only, and then give a new HEEL command and begin walking with your left foot. If these dogs start to lag, quicken your pace slightly, but do not break into a run or you may encourage their aggression.

Remember when dealing with these two dogs to hold the leash close, make light corrections, and verbally praise the dogs all at the same time, to discourage thoughts of biting. Do not run and do not praise them with your hands. The first two days have conditioned these dogs to have considerably more respect for you and to be convinced that you are in control of the situation. You must be careful to keep them thinking this way. Their confidence in you is growing.

Proceed with heeling and right about-turns, stopping every few yards; continue this routine for one ten-minute session before giving a five-minute break. The break should be given on the auxiliary safety line that was used

for the first two days' training and is still attached to a stake. Heel your dog to the long line to which a bolt snap is securely attached. The extra safety collar can be dispensed with now. Just snap on the long line and remove the leash, throwing it out of the circle onto the ground where your dog can see it but not reach it.

Remain in the area, so your dog can see you and touch you if he wants, but not so far in that you would have difficulty removing yourself from his presence should it be necessary. Make sure the area is as distraction-free as possible. After the five-minute break, reinstall the leash, unsnap the line, and heel your dog out of the training area. This ends the third day's training session.

THE FOURTH DAY

The Normal/Average Dog

The normal average dog should be worked as he was on the third day, with the distractions provided at one end of the training area. On this fourth day, instead of removing the distractions on the break, keep them in the area through the break, but take the break at the opposite end of the area from where the distractions are.

Should your dog attempt to make contact with the distractions on this break, you should implement the usual severe right about-turn, grasping the clothesline to your chest, thereby correcting the dog. In addition, any time your dog wanders off more than 12 or 15 feet from you, whether or not it is towards the distraction, he gets a correction. This straying indicates that he is more interested in investigating new things than in watching you. The correction consists of your running two or three feet in the opposite direction from where the dog is heading, and then ignoring him. Repeat this as often as necessary. Remain in the area, saying nothing to your dog and ignoring him completely until you commence to work him for the second 15-minute session. Follow this by another break as outlined above, and then end the session for the fourth day.

The Overfriendly Dog, the High-Strung Dog, the Shy/Fearful Dog, and the Fearful Biter (B)

All these dogs should be worked as the normal/average dog for this fourth day. This includes the continuing distraction at one end of the training area; the distraction should remain on breaks, which should be taken at the opposite end of the training area. All corrections are exactly as for the normal/average dog, which means using the two-handed leash grip.

The Fearful Biter (A) and the Aggressive Dog

These dogs should be worked on the third day with no

Illus. 37. Perfect heel position.

Illus. 38. A close right about-turn correction.

Illus. 40. Praising the dog for heeling.

Illus. 39. The dog coming around with the owner.

distractions. The right about-turns should have been made as hard as necessary within the past three days so the dog is able to tolerate a normal training session today. This consists of two 15-minute sessions, each followed by a five-minute break. This time the breaks should be given on the long line, which is laid out on the ground and ready to be grabbed for about-turn corrections should your dog stray more than 12 to 15 feet from you or charge a distraction. The stake should not be used on the breaks anymore. Continue to praise your dog verbally only; this praise should occur every time you stop and every time you correct him. Continue to say GOOD BOY after you correct him on your right about-turns with the two-handed leash grip. Everything else remains the same.

THE FIFTH DAY

The Normal/Average Dog, the Overfriendly Dog, the High-Strung Dog, and the Aloof Dog

On this fifth day, you are going to introduce some new maneuvers into the established routine. The variations will consist of new directional turns. So far, you've been using only two basic maneuvers: right about-turns and stopping and praising. The right about-turns were 180 degrees, which sent you back in the opposite direction from where you were originally headed. The new turns will consist of 90-degree right- and left-angle turns (Illus. 45–49).

The first turn will be the left-angle turn. It must be understood that these turns must be carried out as clean, crisp, square turns. It will not do to walk in circles or rounded corners. Your dog's attention can best be focused and brought to maximum efficiency if you surprise him with quick, square turns. If your turns are not decisive, the dog's attention can wander as he begins to relax in accordance with your laxity of movement. Another good reason for quick, square turns, is that they make a much more effective correction. So, to keep your dog's attention at optimum peak and to provide the most effective corrections, make square turns. This cannot be overemphasized.

Begin the fifth day by entering your training area as usual with your dog, and proceed to work him as before. The about-turns you have made thus far have kept your dog back so that he won't try to run out in front of you. You might even have found it necessary to run, to keep your dog from lagging as a result of the overeffectiveness of the right about-turn corrections.

At this stage of his training your dog should be heeling at your side, but is probably walking consistently about a head out in front of you. The right about-turn has po-sitioned your dog so he is effectively heeling with you, even though he'd be slightly out in front. More right about-turns will not help to position the dog that extra ten inches or so back that becomes the true, accurate heel posture. To correct this discrepancy in positioning, use the left turn. While heeling your dog, with him once again leading you by about five to ten inches, suddenly make a left turn, pivoting on your left foot, allowing your right knee to tap the dog in the face. Make all left turns into the dog. Make them sharply, abruptly, and without any communication or forewarning from you. After the turn, go back to the usual routine of right about-turns, stops, etc.

The other new maneuver will be a right-angle turn. This is accomplished by pivoting on the left foot and stepping out to the right quickly, sharply, and without communication. The right-angle turn is used to correct the dog when he is heeling wide (which means walking at your side, but too far out to your left). Every time your dog is heeling wide, use the right-angle turn as a correction. Anytime you find your dog heeling slightly ahead of you, the left-angle turn should be used to correct this. The careful and consistent use of these two turns, in addition to the right about-turns, should bring your dog into perfect heel position. Practise this routine, incorporating right- and left-angle turns as needed, working your dog for two 15-minute sessions followed by two five-minute breaks, all with no distractions.

The Shy/Fearful Dog, the Fearful Biter (A and B), and the Aggressive Dog

Work these dogs as the normal/average dog for the fifth day, keeping the dog close, except that the left- and right-angle turns should be made more slowly. The turns should be square, but the impact will not be as severe. These dogs should also be praised with the words GOOD BOY immediately after the corrections. The training should consist of two 15-minute sessions followed by the two 5-minute breaks on the long line. There are no distractions today.

THE SIXTH DAY

All Dogs

All these dogs should be worked as they were on the fifth day of heeling. This includes right about-turns, right-angle turns, left-angle turns, and, when necessary, running to compensate for lagging. The difference for the sixth day is that you should again introduce distractions at one end of the training area. This will be the first day of distractions present during the breaks; take the breaks at the end opposite to the distractions.

Vary your walking pattern, making a series of left- and right-angle turns and right about-turns. React appropriately, according to your dog's response to the distractions. If your dog is right with you, he should receive no corrections as you maneuver him through the turns. Work your dog for two 15-minute sessions followed by two 5-minute breaks, with the distractions present on the breaks. This will end the sixth day's training session for your dog.

THE SEVENTH DAY

All Dogs
All these dogs should be worked as they were on the previous day, except that there should be multiple distractions scattered throughout the area. This could be dogs and cats, adults and children, totalling three or four varied distractions. You could heel your dog throughout this area, getting no closer than eight to ten feet from any distraction, and making any necessary corrections. Take the breaks with the distractions remaining in the area, and take the breaks about 20 feet from the nearest distraction. Two 15-minute sessions followed by the usual two 5-minute breaks will end the seventh day of training.

THE EIGHTH DAY

All Dogs
For all the dogs, the routine will be an exact repetition of the previous day's training.

THE NINTH DAY

All Dogs
All these dogs should now be taken into heavy distractions outside of the training area. The best place would be a shopping center. Your dog must be taken to a place where he does not normally walk, at least two blocks away from your normal work area. Three o'clock is a good time to walk your dog near a school. The children getting out will provide plenty of distractions.

Work your dog for two 15-minute sessions, followed by two controlled five-minute breaks on the six-foot leash, not the long line. After the second five-minute break, heel or drive your dog home. He has now passed the final test of ultimate distractions, and you are to be congratulated for developing a very attentive dog. Your dog is now ready to begin the sit.

Third "Week": The Sit (Illus. 50–54)

The sit is a basic primary command used to control your

dog (Illus. 50). When used with heeling, it is a great way of gaining your dog's attention. When used with the stay, it can change your dog's attitude in a favorable way and can build his confidence in himself and in you.

THE FIRST DAY

The Normal/Average Dog
With no distractions in the training area, begin working your dog on all maneuvers, including right- and left-angle turns and right about-turns. Up to now, you have been praising your dog just for stopping and standing still at your side when you stop. Today, you will begin to change that routine. Holding your dog close to you, with the two-handed leash grip, you should come to a stop. As you do so, let go of the leash with your left hand and continue to hold it only with your right hand.

Now, give the command SIT, prefaced by your dog's name. The command will sound like: DREAM, SIT. Once again, neither bellow nor whisper to your dog; give the command in a clear, emotionless tone. Give the command only once, and immediately force your dog to sit by placing your open left hand on his rear and pushing steadily down, as you exert steady upward pressure on the leash with your right hand (Illus. 51). This upward pressure is not a jerk on the leash, but a steady, strong pressure that will stop the instant your dog is sitting.

Once your dog is sitting, he should receive praise, just as he did in heeling when he stopped and stood at your side. Immediately after the praise you should give a new HEEL command: DREAM, HEEL. There should be no more standing stops as before. On all future stops you should command, DREAM, SIT, and immediately place him on the sit as described above. Continue the routine of heeling, right- and left-angle turns, and right about-turns, stopping every few yards. At every stop, place your dog physically on sits. As soon as he sits, praise him with the words GOOD BOY and proceed with a new HEEL command.

Do not nag your dog with repetitions of SIT, SIT, SIT. Give each command only once, and preface all commands by your dog's name: DREAM, SIT; DREAM, HEEL; etc. Vary your routine of turns and sit placements so as not to become predictable and allow your dog to anticipate your moves. Work him for two 15-minute sessions, followed by two 5-minute breaks with no distractions. This ends the first day's session.

The Overfriendly Dog and the High-Strung Dog
Place these dogs on the sit the same as you did the normal/average dog. The only exception may be that they will not hold the sit very long. They may sit and

Illus. 42. Letting out the leash to its full six feet while quickly making the turn.

Illus. 41. A right about-turn correction. The owner is letting out all the leash, for maximum effect. He has a one-hand grip, preparing for the right about-turn correction.

Illus. 43. The right about-turn. The dog runs out of leash as he and the owner move apart.

Illus. 44. Working an aggressive dog on the safety line.

Illus. 45 and 46 (page 70). Make a left-angle turn to correct the dog when he heels slightly out in front up to one foot.

then hop right up again. If these dogs receive an over-abundance of praise, you will be encouraging such actions. Many of these dogs, when praised, take that praise as their cue to take advantage of you, and they will then jump all over you wildly. If this is the case, you should reduce the amount of praise your dog receives by not praising him physically at all: give only a quick verbal GOOD BOY and immediately move on to a new HEEL command.

The best way to gauge the correct amount of praise to give your dog is to see how much advantage he takes of you when you praise him. As days go by and he becomes more steady and is able to handle more praise, he can get more. In all respects, work your dog through the same routine as for the normal/average dog, with two 15-minute sessions followed by two 5-minute breaks, with no distractions

The Aloof Dog
Place the aloof dog on the sit just as the normal/average dog. He can be given a normal amount of praise. If there is an excessive amount of resistance to being placed, you must increase the upward pressure on the leash; cease the pressure immediately as soon as he sits. Other than that, these dogs should be worked as the normal/average dog with the usual two 15-minute sessions, followed by two 5-minute breaks with no distractions.

The Shy/Fearful Dog, the Fearful Biter (A and B), and the Aggressive Dog
These dogs should be worked just as the normal/average dog, with the exception that, when placing them on the sit, the upward pressure with your right hand should be more gentle and the angle of the leash should be slightly to the front (Illus. 52). In addition, these dogs should be praised with the words GOOD BOY directly after the SIT command, before they are actually sitting. This will lessen their fear and make them go down easier.

Once the dog is sitting, give him a lot of praise, which should now include as much physical praise as possible, before moving on to a new HEEL command. With each new phase of learning, the dogs will react with uncertainty and fear. The best defense against this is effusive praise to diminish their insecurity. Work these dogs as usual, with the two 15-minute sessions followed by the two 5-minute breaks, with no distractions.

THE SECOND DAY

All Dogs
Work all the dogs just as on the first day of placing on sits, with the respective special techniques appropriate to each type of dog.

THE THIRD DAY

The Normal/Average Dog
The normal/average dog can now be placed on sits with multiple distractions present throughout the area. The place you choose can be in or out of your normal work area, as long as the distractions are numerous. Work your dog in the same routine as for the first two days, making the left- and right-angle turns and right about-turns, and running where appropriate. Every few yards, stop, shorten up on the leash, say your dog's name, and then the command SIT. Pull up and press down simultaneously, and praise your dog with the words GOOD BOY. Work him in this routine for the usual two 15-minute sessions, and take the two 5-minute breaks on the long line except in cases where you are out of the normal work area, such as in a shopping center, etc. This completes the third day's session for the normal/average dog.

The Overfriendly Dog and the High-Strung Dog
Work these dogs very firmly on the sit placements, putting steady upward tension on the leash with your right hand and cutting the praise very short. Move on to a new HEEL command quickly. As this approach is repeated again and again, you will begin to see more positive results. The dog is learning that he cannot deter you from your objective with his fancy footwork.

You must understand that your dog's seemingly friendly action of jumping on you when you praise him is really an attempt on his part to put an end to the training session. Work the full routine as described for the normal/average dog, showing him that you do not fall for this ploy. Give him the two 15-minute sessions and the two 5-minute breaks on the long line. If you are working out of your area, such as in a shopping center, take the breaks on the six-foot leash.

The Aloof Dog
The aloof dog should be handled just as the normal/average dog, except that you should continue to vary the routine at such a rapid pace that you excite his interest. If you do not make constant, definitive moves, your stubborn dog will become lethargic and resume his holding back, just as he started to do at the outset of training.

Place him quickly, command him crisply, and praise him lavishly, moving from technique to technique without any lag. In this way, you will leave no time for him to think up ways to resist you. Work your dog for the usual sessions and two 5-minute breaks on the long line, except if you are out of your normal work area; in that case, use the six-foot leash for the breaks.

The Shy/Fearful Dog

Work this dog just as the normal/average dog, except that your praise with the words GOOD BOY should be given while you are placing the dog as well as after placing him. Praise him lavishly. Work two 15-minute sessions, followed by two 5-minute breaks on the long line. If you are out of your normal work area, take the breaks on the six-foot leash.

The Fearful Biter (A and B) and the Aggressive Dog

These dogs should be placed on sits in the same manner as the normal/average dog, except that, with the larger breeds, the tension should be straight up on the leash. Your fist should rotate towards your face, and your right forearm should bend close into your body, blocking your face and vital parts from your dog's mouth. With the smaller dogs, the leash grip should be shortened and the tension should be directed towards the front of the dog and away from you. The pressure on the rump remains the same with both sizes of dogs.

Do not forget to praise your dog with the words GOOD BOY as you place him and directly after the command. Keep the right-hand leash tension gentle and release it immediately as your dog sits. Your praise should continue to be physical as well as verbal, for the more you can touch your dog the more confident it will make him in you. If your dog seems nervous and starts to show aggression, return to verbal praise only.

Work the dog for two 15-minute sessions with the two 5-minute breaks on the long line, unless your work area is very public and is a difficult place in which to exercise control. In this case, the six-foot leash should be used for the breaks.

THE FOURTH DAY

All Dogs

All of the dogs should be worked just as they were on the third day of sit placement, with distractions. You should also concentrate on the heeling, to obtain maximum precision placement of your dog in the heel position. With every new technique, constant reinforcement is necessary with the familiar material to maintain peak performance and accuracy. Work your dog for the usual two 15-minute sessions, with the controlled five-minute breaks on the long line or the six-foot leash, depending upon what the situation requires.

THE FIFTH DAY

All Dogs

Work all the dogs just as you did on the third and fourth days of sit placement. They should again be placed on sits during multiple distractions. Continue working on obedience for each move, and vary the routine so that your dog does not predict your movements or commands.

If you are having any difficulty in executing square right and left turns, both of which require you to pivot on the left foot, work through the motions without the dog until your footwork is very secure. Continue to train yourself in quick counterresponses to whatever mistakes in heeling position your dog may succumb to. As these are repeated, your trigger-quick responses should become second nature to you, and you will always be ensured of a perfect heel position from your dog. Work the dog for the two 15-minute sessions followed by the two 5-minute breaks, either on the long line or on the six-foot leash, depending on the work area you have chosen.

THE SIXTH DAY

The Normal/Average Dog and the Overfriendly Dog

With absolutely no distractions in the training area, enter the area, heeling your dog with a slightly shortened two-handed leash grip. Begin heeling your dog and, as you walk, prepare yourself mentally for your next stop. No longer will you place your dog and no longer will you tell him to sit. You should say nothing as you stop. Just remain ready, as you now come to a complete stop. If your dog sits, praise him. If your dog does not, correct him in the following manner: Without saying a word, and still gripping the leash with both hands, jerk with all your might straight upward above the dog and towards your right shoulder (Illus. 53). Do not say SIT. Do not say NO. Just give one terrifically hard correction. The correction should be so hard and forceful that it actually forces your dog into the sit position.

If your dog sits at this time, praise him with the words GOOD BOY. If your dog is not sitting by this time, the fault is not his but yours in that you have undercorrected him by not jerking hard enough. If this is the case, you should now give a vocal SIT command, such as DREAM, SIT. If he sits, praise him. If not, you should then correct him again in a similar manner, only much harder this time, so as to force him into the sit position with your correction.

The correction should be given in approximation to the size of the dog. If your dog sits after this correction, praise him with the words GOOD BOY. Should your dog, for some reason, still remain standing and refuse to sit, you are definitely undercorrecting him. Most dogs respond to one or two proper corrections. Your task is to alternate a correction and a command for as long as is

Illus. 46. Make a sharp left-angle turn into the dog.

Illus. 47–49. Make a right-angle turn to correct the dog when it heels wide away from you.

Illus. 48. The right-angle-turn correction.

Illus. 49. The dog once again heeling alongside his trainer.

necessary to make your dog sit. This exercise must only end one way, with your dog sitting.

Do not approach the correction with the fear that you may be hurting your dog. You will not. The dog must have a correction that will be memorable for him for the rest of his life, so that he will perform reliably in ultimate distractions and in any given situation. The five days of placement have adequately prepared him for what you expect from him, so a very forceful correction is justified. Though this method may appear harsh, in reality it is the kindest method and causes the least amount of punishment to your dog.

Remember to correct your dog silently, wait a few seconds, and give a new command: DREAM, SIT. Then wait a few seconds and give another silent, hard correction. Be careful not to say SIT as you are correcting him. The correction and command must be kept separate. The few seconds wait between actions is to give your dog a chance to sit, thereby receiving his reward—your praise. Praise your dog whether he sits on the correction or on the command. He is being praised for sitting. How he got there is incidental to the praise. Finally, by whatever means is needed, your dog is sitting.

Directly after the praise, move on to a new HEEL command. Make another definitive stop and wait a second or two to give your dog a chance to react. Most dogs will sit after the initial introduction to the sit correction. Should your dog decide not to sit, promptly react with another forceful, silent sit correction. If he sits this time praise him and move on to a new HEEL command: DREAM, HEEL. If he does not sit, give him a new SIT command, and keep alternating, as before, with corrections and commands until he does sit. Plan your stops and make them crisp and decisive. Where you decide to stop is where your dog must sit. Remember that, should your dog not sit upon your stop, the silent correction comes first, not the SIT command (Illus. 54).

Work your dog in the established routine of heeling with all turns. This time you should have an automatic sit on every stop instead of the previous sit placement. Never go back to placing your dog on sits now that he has received the sit correction. You no longer have to show your dog what you want; you now have only to enforce it every time you stop. Your dog may attempt to take advantage of you if you are involved in other things.

Never tell your dog to do anything unless you are able to enforce it, and that means the leash and collar must be on for now. Resist the temptation to show off the results of the obedience training to your friends until you and the dog are firmly entrenched in each new routine and able to handle great distractions. Work your dog in the usual two 15-minute sessions, without distractions,

and take the two 5-minute breaks on the long line, also without distractions.

The High-Strung Dog
The high-strung dog should be worked just as the normal/average dog, with the exception that you may find him taking a few steps around in front of you and sitting there. This shows that he is trying to cooperate but is a little confused as to where he should sit. A further teaching process is needed to solve this specific problem. It should be corrected now before it is repeated too many times. Anything that is repeated in dog training is learned, whether it be right or wrong. Therefore, you must correct any errors in positioning before they become habits. Whether your dog is swinging his rear out and facing you, or whether he walks around a few steps in front of you and then sits facing you, both positions are wrong and must be corrected. Correct these mistakes by making all of your stops against a wall, a tree, a fence, or any such available object so as to prevent your dog from swinging his rear out sideways. The next technique should be to quicken your leash corrections for the automatic sit, so that the dog has no choice but to sit immediately at your side where he stops. Thus, he is receiving the correction before he has time to take the two or three extra steps that will bring him around in front of you. Both techniques will be most effective when used together.

The Aloof Dog
The aloof dog should be treated just as the normal/average dog, with good hard corrections and no coaxing or pleading. This dog usually requires a few extra corrections, which must be consistently very hard to discourage further resistance. This dog has enough natural resistance built in, so we don't want to encourage any more.

Once the aloof dog is sitting, he may renew his reluctance to walk with you. Your response to this should be to break into short runs as before, until he is once again walking at your side and sitting when you stop. The dog's technique is to try to fool or bluff his owner into thinking that he really doesn't know what is expected of him. But if you have followed the day-by-day procedure as outlined in this book, you can rest assured that he knows exactly what you want. You must have patience to outlast his stubbornness. Continue with the routine until he reacts properly.

The Shy/Fearful Dog
The shy/fearful dog should be treated as the normal/average dog, except that there should be plenty of praise once he is sitting. He should respond very well to the sit

corrections and require very few of them. This dog may also sit sideways or sit out in front like the high-strung dog. To counteract these tendencies, use the two methods—heeling alongside a solid object and very quick corrections—as outlined in detail for the high-strung dog.

The shy/fearful dog may also overreact to the sit correction by lying down. This is caused by fear. He lies down in submission. Once again, this behavior is a mistake and, if repeated, is learned, So, it must be stopped immediately. To prevent it, as you come to a stop, shorten up on your leash grip and verbally praise your dog with the words GOOD BOY as he starts to sit. At the same time, tighten up on the leash tension, not allowing the dog to lie down, and continue praising him as he sits. The praise will help to allay the fear that is causing him to lie down. If he remains sitting, you may physically praise him with your left hand on top of his head for a few seconds before giving him a new HEEL command.

If, when you stop, your dog is still trying his best to lie down, then, immediately after a quick GOOD BOY, heel him off again by saying his name and the command HEEL. Your praise must be fast enough to be dispensed before he starts to lie down. This quick praising and immediate moving off with a new HEEL command does not give him the time to lie down. As this is repeated, you are creating an environment where he is not able to lie down but, conversely, is repeating the correct thing and thereby building up his confidence. If your dog responds to the sit correction by refusing to walk, you should correct him by breaking into short runs at frequent intervals.

With the shy/fearful dog, every new phase of training will bring a temporary setback to his confidence but, as each new command is learned and repeated, his confidence will be built back up again. This very positive approach to training the shy/fearful dog will actually build his self-confidence, where nagging, coaxing methods will produce a more frightened dog that will do his obedience poorly and unreliably at best.

The Fearful Biter (A and B) and the Aggressive Dog

Reinstall the stake and safety line as previously used in the first two days of heeling. Begin heeling your dog counterclockwise around the stake, at the end of the safety line. Heel him around two complete circles and then make your first stop.

For the first stop only, place the dog on a sit. This should be the last placement for these dogs. Give a HEEL command immediately and start walking once around the circle, making sure you are at the end of the safety-line tension. Now, make your stop and give the

verbal command by calling your dog's name and commanding him to SIT. Give the command clearly and firmly, and give it only once. If your dog sits, praise him and move on with a new HEEL command. If not, correct him in the following manner: Exactly three seconds after giving your command, jerk straight up so forcefully that it forces your dog to sit. This correction should be done silently.

If your dog now sits, you should praise him and move on with a new HEEL command. If he does not, remain standing where you are and repeat the command: DREAM, SIT. Three seconds later, again correct in a strong upward direction, with both your hands on the leash. He should now be sitting. You should praise him and walk on with a new HEEL command.

Continue this routine of a command and a correction until your dog is sitting on command. Remember to make your corrections very, very hard. This will discourage your dog from resisting you and minimize the corrections he will have to take. Walk on with a new HEEL command, and halfway around the circle make another stop. Again, give the command: DREAM, SIT. If he sits, praise him. If not, give the correction, and continue alternating in this manner until he does sit.

Keep making very hard corrections, and continue to keep just within the outer perimeter of the safety line. Give him one 15-minute session of this, followed by a five-minute break on a spare long line that will be lying on the ground in the work area, with a bolt snap securely attached. Unsnap the staked line, snap on the long line, and then unsnap the leash and toss it on the ground, telling your dog, OKAY, THAT'S ALL, and letting him walk freely on the long line for his break.

For the second 15-minute session, snap on the leash, release the auxiliary long line, take your dog to the safety stake, snap on the safety line, and begin heeling in a counterclockwise circle as before. Give the HEEL command and begin walking. Complete two rotations around the circle and then stop. Wait three seconds and then, if your dog is not sitting, say nothing and give him a very hard physical correction as before, in an upward direction. If he sits, praise him and walk on, giving a new HEEL command.

On your next stop, repeat the procedure: the silent stop, and, three seconds later, the correction, if needed. Once your dog sits, praise him and walk on. You now have accomplished the automatic sit. Your dog should be sitting by your side without a command each time you stop. After this second session of 15 minutes, give him another break with the auxiliary clothesline dragging on the ground. This will end the training session for the day.

Illus. 50. The sit-at-heel position.

Illus. 51. Placing the dog on the sit command.

Illus. 53. The sit correction. Correct the dog towards your right shoulder.

Illus. 52. Placing an aggressive dog on the sit command. When a forearm block and safety line are used, the face and other vital areas are better protected.

If, while your dog is first being corrected, he attempts to bite you, you should lift quickly, straight upwards with both hands on the leash, while using the leverage of the safety line to prevent the dog from reaching you and to help control him. Bellow the single word NO! as you lift and hold him up in the air. Do not put him down until he stops all aggressive action. Then repeat the command, DREAM, SIT. Should he not sit, you should administer a very severe sit correction, which will be silent, and alternate command with correction until he does sit. If he attempts again to bite you, again lift him straight up in the air, raising your dog off the ground and bellowing another loud NO! Hold him up until he halts all aggression and longs to be back on all fours again. Command him to sit again, DREAM, SIT, and praise him verbally when he does so, quickly moving on to another new HEEL command.

Remember that there are two corrections: one jerking correction for not sitting and one lifting and holding-up correction for attempting to bite you. You must administer the proper correction for each mistake. Also remember that the correction for not sitting is done silently, whereas the correction for attempting to bite is a very loud, verbal NO, as well as physically lifting the dog in the air. Should you find it necessary to administer the lifting correction, it is highly important that you do not let time elapse after the correction in which you do nothing or get sudden pangs of guilt and decide to pet your dog to assuage your conscience for the terrible thing you think you have just done to him. Immediately give a new SIT command. The SIT command is issued rather than the HEEL command because until he has sat, even with corrections, the command is not yet over. Once he is sitting, you can give quick verbal praise and move on to a new HEEL command. Rarely will you find more than two lifting corrections necessary if you have done them properly, and most often one will suffice.

Continue with your training program, walking counterclockwise and administering the proper commands as though nothing unusual has occurred. You should be getting automatic sits every time now. If you don't, you know what to do. Remember, do not tell your dog SIT anymore, except if after a needed correction he still is not sitting.

THE SEVENTH DAY

The Normal/Average Dog, the Overfriendly Dog, the High-Strung Dog, the Aloof Dog, and the Shy/Fearful Dog

Work all these dogs as they were worked on the sixth day, enforcing the automatic sit at all times. Today, you should introduce a distraction at one end of the work area and enter the area from the opposite side, continuing to work your way towards the distraction. Now you have two ways of commanding your dog's attention over a distraction: if your dog's attention starts to focus on the distraction, simply stop walking immediately and your dog should sit quickly. If he does not sit quickly, an immediate sit correction should refocus his attention upon you. So, now you can use both the right about-turn as well as the automatic sit to gain your dog's quick attention in a distracting situation. He is learning that a distraction is both a trap for him and the signal to become extra-attentive to your movements and commands.

Work your dog for the usual two 15-minute sessions, with the subsequent two 5-minute breaks on the long line (Illus. 55). The distractions should remain present on the breaks. This ends the seventh day for your dog.

The Fearful Biter and the Aggressive Dog

Bring your dog out and hook him to the stake. Start heeling him around the stake on the safety line. After two complete revolutions, make your stop. Say nothing. If your dog sits, verbally praise him. If he does not sit, correct him with a hard jerk; give praise once he is sitting. Then move on with a new HEEL command. When he has made three automatic sits on consecutive stops, or has taken three consecutive corrections and then sat after them, he is ready to be worked off the safety line.

Unsnap the bolt, leaving the extra chain collar hanging loosely around his neck. It is very important that there be no distractions in your work area, as your dog can renew his resistance at an inopportune moment for you. The progress and conditioning of your fearful biter or aggressive dog must advance in very gradual stages. Skipping a stage by prematurely introducing uncontrollable distractions will make enforcement much more difficult for you and could cause a completely unnecessary setback in your dog's training progress. He is convinced from the first day's corrections that you can enforce what you require of him. Be sure to keep him thinking that way. Gradually, he should be so completely convinced of your capability that he won't even think about contesting your will. This will happen, but it happens slowly and in stages.

Once your dog is able to take sit corrections from you, he is able to join the other dogs and work in distractions. Work him for two 15-minute sessions, following each with a five-minute break on the long line. Take your dog off the stake for the breaks as well as for the work sessions. There should be no distractions during the breaks either.

THE EIGHTH DAY

The Normal/Average Dog, the Overfriendly Dog, the High-Strung Dog, the Aloof Dog, and the Shy/Fearful Dog

Today, again work all of these dogs with distractions, using both the automatic sit as well as the right about-turns to keep your dog's attention upon you. Take them to a shopping center or crowded street and work with multiple distractions. Do not allow children or adults walking by to make contact with your dog, and don't get into any conversations with passersby. People may be interested in what you are doing, but you will lose control over the situation if you indulge their interest. Do not be afraid to correct your dogs as hard as necessary, even though some people may say something about your "brutality."

Work your dog for one 20-minute session with no break, and then walk or drive him home.

The Fearful Biter and the Aggressive Dog

Today, these dogs should be worked off the safety line, and a distraction should be introduced at one end of the training area. You should work your dog towards and then away from the distraction, in the usual manner, employing the right about-turns and the automatic sits to command your dog's attention over the distraction. Enter the training area opposite to the distraction, continuing to work your dog towards it. Never come closer to the distraction than ten feet.

Vary your commands by stopping abruptly, thereby enforcing the automatic sit, and making right about-turns requiring your dog to come around with you. If you want more critical attention from your dog, make more frequent stops. You can walk as little as one or two steps and still require another automatic sit. If your dog seems very interested in the distraction, your constant stops will require so much of his attention that his interest in the distraction will soon wane.

Work your dog for two 15-minute sessions, followed by two 5-minute breaks on the long line. The distraction should remain present, but your breaks are taken at the opposite end of the work area from the distraction.

THE NINTH DAY

The Normal/Average Dog, the Overfriendly Dog, the High-Strung Dog, the Aloof Dog, and the Shy/Fearful Dog

All these dogs should again be worked with heavy distractions at a shopping center, etc., just as in the previous day's training. This is the ultimate in distractions, and your dog should be working well for you by this time.

Work your dog for one 20-minute session today, with no break. Your dog is now ready to begin learning the Stay command.

The Fearful Biter and the Aggressive Dog

These dogs should now be worked with heavy distractions at a shopping center. This is a multiple-distraction situation that is the most difficult for your dog to overcome. It is vitally important that you, as well as your dog, ignore the distractions completely. Do not converse with curiosity seekers or react to comments by passersby. Above all, do not allow people to pet your dog. This situation takes every bit of your control and attention. In order to accomplish your goals, don't allow anything to interfere with your efforts or it will diminish your results.

This ninth day of work must be repeated for two additional days with heavy distractions, making a total of 11 days on sits. Each session will be 20 minutes in duration, with no breaks. For these two categories of dogs, a total of three days in heavy distractions should prepare them sufficiently so that they should now be ready to begin learning the stay command.

Fourth "Week": The Sit-Stay (Illus. 56–72)

THE FIRST DAY

The Normal/Average Dog

On this first day of the sit-stay, there will be no distractions used (Illus. 56). Enter the training area with your dog on the leash and begin your heeling routine as usual. Work your dog with the customary stops, automatic sits, and the usual turns. After two or three minutes, when your dog is thoroughly warmed up and working well, you are ready to begin the mechanics of teaching him to stay.

Begin heeling your dog. As you come to a complete stop and he is sitting by your side, let go of the leash with your left hand but continue holding it with your right. Swing your left hand across your body, with your palm facing your dog and your fingers open (Illus. 57). Your hand should move slowly towards his face, stopping about three inches from his nose. This action should be accompanied by your referring to your dog's name and commanding him to stay.

You should now leave your dog by stepping out in front of him with your right foot. Pivot on your right foot, so you are now facing the dog. Still facing your dog, step back with your right foot and take a second step with your left, drawing it alongside your right foot. You should maintain the stay signal with your left hand, as

Illus. 54. The automatic sit.

Illus. 55. Take time for a break with your dog.

78

Illus. 56. The sit-stay.

Illus. 57–60 (pages 82 and 83). The sit-stay command and hand signal.

79

you also maintain an upward tension on the leash with your right hand (Illus. 58).

After three seconds have elapsed, you should immediately return to the heel position by stepping back to your dog's side with your left foot and pivoting on your left heel clockwise as you then step back with your right foot (Illus. 59). As soon as you have returned to the heel position, take up the leash properly, promptly releasing the tension on the leash and praising your dog with the words GOOD BOY (Illus. 60). Move off with a new HEEL command and vary the routine, doing a couple of automatic sits.

Now you are ready to try another sit-stay. Make another stop. Let go of the leash with your left hand, and give the STAY command and hand signal as before. Repeating the same footwork as before, leave your dog, and step out and face him as you maintain the tension on the leash with your right hand. With your left hand, maintain the stay signal in front of his face.

Return to your dog's side, as previously described, and praise him. Then begin walking with a new HEEL command: DREAM, HEEL. Continue working your dog on this complete routine, implementing the sit-stay about every third stop, or approximately every minute. Work your dog with no distractions for the usual two 15-minute sessions followed by the two 5-minute breaks. This will end the first day's training on the sit-stay.

It is important to mention at this time that the STAY command should be given only once, and not repeated in a nagging manner. There should be no need to repeat the command because your dog is not able to break (get up from) the stay at this time. The tension exerted on the leash with your right hand holds the dog in place, making it impossible for him to get up. Also, the brief period of time that your dog is on the stay (two to three seconds) does not even give him enough time to think about breaking. Both of these safeguards, the upward tension and the short period of time, will be maintained throughout the entire first lesson.

The Overfriendly Dog and the High-Strung Dog
Both of these dogs will have more of a tendency to break the stay than any of the other dogs. The key to success with these dogs will be to make certain that they are not able to break the stay. This is done, again, with very short stays and increased upward tension on the leash, holding your dog firmly in place. If the dog overreacts to your physical praise when you return by jumping around, dispense with physical praise and reduce the verbal praise to a very quick GOOD BOY, immediately followed by a new HEEL command.

The Aloof Dog
The aloof dog is worked just like the normal/average dog, with no deviation in routine.

The Shy/Fearful Dog
Work the shy/fearful dog like the normal/average dog, but give him effusive praise on the return. Very short stays will make things easier for dogs in this category.

The Fearful Biter and the Aggressive Dog
These dogs should be worked like the normal/average dog, except that you should considerably curtail the sweep of your hand on the stay signal. Make only a very moderate gesture, holding your hand an inch or two from your body or use verbal commands only (Illus. 61). Never push your hand into the dog's face; this could be misconstrued by your dog as aggression on your part. Keep your palm open but close to your body while maintaining the signal with your left hand and the upward tension with your right hand. When you return, give verbal praise only; begin dispensing the praise as you are returning rather than wait until you are back at the heel position. This should serve to dispel his apprehension.

Do not run back to your dog's side as you return, but return slowly, praising him verbally as you do so. Once you are back at heel position, move on to a new HEEL command and take your dog through his complete routine, including frequent stays (every 60 seconds approximately), for two 15-minute sessions followed by two 5-minute breaks, all with no distractions.

THE SECOND DAY

The Normal/Average Dog
Enter the training area with your dog on the leash. Begin taking him through his paces, just as you did on the first day of the sit-stay. Begin by making stops, enforcing the automatic sit if necessary. As your dog gets into the work routine, prepare for your next stop, which will be a sit-stay. Leave your dog as before (Illus. 62). Step out with the described footwork and turn facing your dog. Continue holding the stay signal while maintaining tension on the leash with your right hand. After two or three seconds return to heel position, take up the leash, and then praise your dog. Move on with a new HEEL command.

After a few more stops with just an automatic sit, again command your dog by saying his name and STAY, giving the proper accompanying hand signal. Move out in front of your dog, this time releasing the upward tension on the leash and also dropping your hand to your side

(Illus. 63). Count five seconds to yourself; then immediately return to your dog's side, take up the leash, and praise him. Continue working your dog on his complete routine and prepare for another sit-stay.

Again leave your dog, call his name and command him to STAY, and give the signal. Move out in front, releasing the tension on the leash and dropping your hand to your side. Remain standing motionless and watching your dog for another five seconds (Illus. 64). Again return to your dog's side, after having given the signal. Work this way for the first 15 minutes. After this practice, give your dog his usual break on the long line.

After the break, switch once again to the leash and begin heeling your dog across the training area. Come to a stop. Give the STAY command and signal. Leave your dog with the usual footwork. Remember to drop the hand signal once again and release the tension on the leash. When you are out in front, smoothly step back one step and remain standing motionless for five seconds. Return to your dog's side, take up the leash, and praise him (Illus. 65 and 66).

Continue working the complete routine, interspersing stays at regular intervals. The second 15-minute work session differs from the first only in the respect that you should back up one step once you are in front of your dog. The stay should still be held for five seconds, and you should always take up the leash with the proper hand grip before praising your dog. This will teach him to remain holding the stay after you return to him. He must wait until you signal, by your praise, that he is released. After the second 15-minute work session, take the usual five-minute break on the long line and end the lesson for this second day of sit-stays for your normal/average dog.

The Overfriendly Dog and the High-Strung Dog

These dogs should be worked just as the normal/average dog, with the exception that you should give only verbal praise and, upon returning, hesitate an extra two or three seconds before praising them. It is very important that you give the command and hand signal only once. Do not nag the dog with repetitive commands and signals. The clearer and louder your command is given, the longer it will last in your dog's mind.

It is very important when working these types of dogs that you do not convey to them an excited form of behavior on your part. Go through every routine with a calm, methodical approach. An excited demeanor would mirror your dog's behavior, and would only serve to make him more high-strung or overexuberant. Your dog is looking for an excuse to become very excited and end the work session. Don't let your mannerisms provide this avenue of escape for him.

The Aloof Dog

The aloof dog is worked just like the normal/average dog for this second day of teaching the stay.

The Shy/Fearful Dog

The shy/fearful dog should be worked the same as the normal/average dog on this second day of stays. The differences should continue to be effusive praise on your return and even slight verbal praise while you are returning, to build up the dog's confidence. This dog can even be praised verbally while he is heeling as you are walking if you feel his excessive apprehension warrants it.

The Fearful Biter and the Aggressive Dog

These dogs should be worked the same as the normal/average dog. Continue the hand signal in close proximity to your body. Praise your dog verbally only. If he appears tense, also praise him verbally as you are returning. Work your dog in a calm, precise manner. Never make jerky, excited movements or use rash vocal inflections. You would only serve to increase his apprehension and aggressive tendencies.

Do not be afraid if your dog appears nervous when you introduce a new procedure into the routine. As the new work is repeated and learned more thoroughly, you will notice your dog becoming more relaxed and confident, both in himself and in you. This is precisely what you are aiming to achieve. The usual two 15-minute sessions, with the accompanying five-minute breaks on the long line, will end this second day of stays for your dog.

THE THIRD DAY
The Normal/Average Dog

Begin working your dog as usual with the complete routine as a warmup. Then come to a stop; he should automatically sit. Put him on a stay and leave him by stepping out one foot away. Wait five seconds, return to the heel position, take up the leash, and praise him.

After a couple of stops where you praised your dog for just sitting, come to a stop and leave him on a stay. This time you will leave differently. Give the STAY command as usual, with your left hand in front of your dog's face. Then leave your dog by confidently walking from him, letting out the full six feet of the leash behind you. When you reach the end of the six feet, slowly turn and face your dog. Stand facing your dog and remain motionless as you count off three seconds. Be certain not to exert any pressure on the leash; it must be slack. Then smoothly return to the heel position at your dog's side, taking up the leash with the proper hand grip, and praise him. Then move on with a new HEEL command.

If your dog chooses to break the sit-stay by getting up

Illus. 58. Step out in front with your right foot, maintaining tension on the leash.

Illus. 59. The trainer returning to heel position.

Illus. 61. The stay signal for aggressive dogs consists of sometimes only using verbal commands.

Illus. 60. Take up the leash and praise your dog.

and attempting to walk away while you are leaving him on the stay, when you are out at the six-foot distance on the leash, or as you are returning to his side at heel position, correct him in the following manner. In order to break the sit-stay, before the dog can walk away from the spot he has been sitting on he must first stand up from the sit position. It is at this precise moment, as his rear end is lifted up off the floor, that he must be corrected (Illus. 67)—not later, after he has taken several steps away from you or in your direction. As his rear comes off the floor and as he attempts to break the sit-stay, even before he has a chance to take the first step in any direction, you should promptly correct him from wherever you are by sharply jerking on the leash, accompanied by a simultaneous verbal NO.

The correction should not propel your dog towards you. It should be so quick, in a sharp jerk and release motion, that your dog sits right back down on the very spot that he attempted to move from. In this way, you will be able to correct your dog from the full six feet away.

After the correction, if your dog is still not sitting, he should receive a new SIT-STAY command, with the appropriate hand signal (Illus. 68). You should alternate in this way with correction, command, correction, command until he is sitting. You can then return to the dog's side and praise him.

Remember, you are correcting your dog at precisely the same moment that he attempts to break the stay. This could be as you are leaving him on a stay, while you are out at the full six feet, or upon your return to heel position. This will teach your dog that you don't need to be right near him to correct him, and if he realizes this he will feel secure while holding his stay.

If, upon your return, your dog gets up before you praise him, you will have to correct him with the usual jerk and release, coupled with the word NO. It is very undesirable to have to correct a dog that has successfully maintained a sit-stay and chooses to break on your return. There are certain techniques that will help you to keep him sitting as you return. Don't run back to your dog's side quickly, taking up the leash with a quick, excited, jerking motion. This will only tend to make him get up, and this would really not be his fault. Instead, as you return to the dog, slow down your pace and move to his side with a slow, controlled motion. Similarly, take up the leash in the same calm, methodical fashion. Your dog should tend to emulate your controlled attitude on your return, and this will help to keep him sitting.

The way you return to your dog is very important, and the order in which you do things upon your return is also very important. You should first return to your dog's side

at heel position, with him on your left. Then take up the leash slowly, with the proper hand grip, and, finally, praise your dog. Remember, once he has been praised, he is allowed to stand up, so make sure you have the proper leash grip before you praise him; then you are ready to move on immediately to a new HEEL command should he get up while you are praising him. The basic method employed in this training is to slowly build up the dog on the stays, instead of making him stay for an extended period of time and correcting him when he breaks the stay. With this method you are trying to accomplish the teaching process with as few corrections as possible, so you can justify the firm corrections once your dog fully understands what is expected of him.

Move on to a new HEEL command and work your dog on a few automatic sits. Then, try a sit-stay, leaving your dog for five seconds at the full six feet. Return in the proper manner, take up the leash, and praise him. Do not try any stays longer than five seconds at this time. Continue working on the heeling, sits, and sit-stays for both 15-minute periods of this day's training. Give your dog the usual five-minute breaks on the long line, between the two work sessions and at the end, with distractions. Take him to the front or back of the house, depending upon which location provides greater distractions. However, it is very important that there are *no* distractions during today's work sessions.

The Overfriendly Dog and the High-Strung Dog
These dogs should be worked just like the normal/average dog, except that special attention should be given to the return with these dogs because they are most likely to break upon your return. Smooth, controlled return, as previously described for the normal/average dog, will produce maximum results with these dogs. If they should break in spite of everything you do, you should correct them in the usual way. Say NO, jerk on the leash, and then repeat the commands SIT, STAY.

Another danger spot with dogs in these two categories is their inability to accept praise in a rational way. They overreact to the praise, jumping all over you or attempting to run away. You can counteract this by quickly praising your dog verbally only and immediately moving on to a new HEEL command. As this is repeated, he will see that he cannot take advantage of you and will not attempt his wild antics any longer. Later on, as he is able to accept your praise with control, you should be able to increase the verbal praise and even some physical praise as well. By your dog's actions you can judge how much praise he should receive. If he goes wild or jumps all over you, cut down the praise to a level where he no longer reacts in this manner.

Train your dog for the usual two 15-minute sessions,

without distractions, followed by the two 5-minute breaks on the long line, with distractions.

The Aloof Dog

The aloof dog should be worked like the normal/average dog and corrected forcefully if he attempts to break. This dog, in particular, may look away from you when you give the STAY command. This might lead you to believe that you should give the hand signal to accommodate where he happens to be looking. Wrong! Your responsibility is to give the command; his is to see it. So don't worry where your dog is looking. If he doesn't stay, just correct him firmly.

Your dog may also look away while on the sit-stay, or perhaps even face the other direction. Give your commands and make your corrections as if your dog were watching you, and eventually he will be. Remember, he doesn't get corrected for looking away, but for getting up from the stay.

Work your dog for the usual two 15-minute sessions, with no distractions, followed by the two 5-minute breaks on the long line, with distractions. This will end the third day on the sit-stay for this dog.

The Shy/Fearful Dog

The shy/fearful dog should be treated just like the normal/average dog. It is very important that you do not put this dog in the position of being corrected on the sit-stay. Leave him for only three seconds, thereby building his confidence and minimizing corrections. If this dog starts to shake nervously, move, or lie down as you start to return, a very quiet, reassuring, VERY GOOD, JUST RELAX, will help to allay his fears. The reassuring sound of your voice will build his confidence, rather than the silence that allows him to succumb to his innate fear.

Once you reach his side, lavishly praise him both physically and verbally (Illus. 69). Whether your dog is shy and afraid because of his breeding or because of mistreatment, he is probably most afraid when someone approaches close to him, and your return from the stay will be an anxious moment for him. As your return, with the accompanying praise, is repeated, your dog's confidence will grow and this will begin to change his attitude. In each case, with each different command, be it SIT, STAY, DOWN, or HEEL, the important thing is not only to teach your dog the mechanics of each command, but to do it in such a way as to improve the dog's attitude favorably and change his personality more towards that of the normal/average dog.

Work your dog for the usual two 15-minute sessions, without distractions, followed by the two 5-minute breaks, with distractions. This ends the third day of the sit-stay for the shy/fearful dog.

The Fearful Biter and the Aggressive Dog.

These dogs should be worked like the shy/fearful dog. This will mean praising them verbally as you return. These dogs' problems, in almost all cases, have been caused by abuse rather than inferior breeding, so they will be especially apprehensive as you return from the stay. Offer soft verbal praise as you draw near, and carry your hands low. Return to your dog in the following manner: Instead of approaching directly in line with your dog and swinging into heel position, slowly make a wide swing and bypass your dog, making him feel you are going to walk right past him, and then smoothly and slowly return to heel position. This will minimize the dog's fears about your return and, in this way, build up his confidence and trust in you. Praise both types of dogs physically as soon as possible. If they allow you to touch them, this indicates their attitude is beginning to improve.

Work these dogs for two 15-minute sessions, without distractions, followed by two 5-minute breaks on the long line, with distractions. This ends the third day on the stay for these dogs.

THE FOURTH DAY

Normal/Average Dog

Bring your dog into the training area. Start working him in his general routine of heeling, automatic sits, and right and left turns, reviewing everything he does. After a few minutes, when he is warmed up and working well, come to a stop. Give the STAY command and signal, and leave your dog, taking off on your right foot. Walk to the full six-foot length of the leash, and turn and face him. After 15 seconds, return to the heel position at your dog's side, take up the leash with the proper hand positions, and then praise your dog. Again, move on with a new HEEL command, taking off on your left foot (Illus. 70). In fact, any time you want the dog to walk with you, take off on your left foot; this is the foot closest to him when you are at correct heel position, and he can notice it more easily. When you want the dog to stay, leave him by taking off starting with your right foot (Illus. 71); this is the foot farthest from him, making it less likely that he would move out with you.

On your next stop, just praise your dog when he sits, and then move on with a new HEEL command. Come to a stop, and when your dog sits give the STAY command and leave him in the usual manner. Remember to give the command and signals properly and with the

Illus. 62–66. The final sequence of the sit-stay command consists of the stay hand signal and command.

Illus. 63. Walking out to the full six feet of leash.

Illus. 64. Out in front of the dog at the full six-foot distance.

Illus. 65. The trainer slowly returning to heel position.

Illus. 66. Take up the leash and praise the dog.

name: for example, DREAM, STAY. Give the hand signal simultaneously as you speak his name, and then the word STAY, expecting your dog to comply. Leave, walking the full six feet away, and turn around and face your dog for 15 seconds. If your dog should break, correct him from the full six feet away with a sharp jerk and release, coupled with the word NO! Then return to his side, take up the leash, and praise him.

Continue working the dog, alternating every other stop with a sit-stay. All sit-stays should be 15 seconds in duration; make corrections when necessary. The session should be the normal 15 minutes, but note that there should be no distractions on this fourth day of the sit-stay.

Give your dog the usual five-minute break on the long line, with distractions. Then begin working your dog as before, except that the length of the stays should be increased to 25 seconds. Work your dog for a second 15-minute session, followed by another five-minute break on the long line, with distractions.

The Overfriendly Dog and the High-Strung Dog
Work these dogs like the normal/average dog, being careful not to overpraise them. Give them only as much praise as they can handle. Remember to move out on your right foot after having given the STAY command and signal. When giving a new HEEL command, take off on your left foot, the one closest to the dog.

Work your dog for one 15-minute session, on his whole routine, using 15-second stays, followed by a five-minute break on the long line, with distractions. The second session should be the same as the first, except that the stays are increased to 25 seconds. Work your dog without distractions for both sessions, and introduce distractions only on the breaks.

The Aloof Dog
Work the aloof dog like the normal/average dog, except that you must be sure to give your commands and signals in the proper way. Sometimes these dogs will renew their stubbornness and try to resist walking with you as a new command is presented to them. Your reaction to this apparent lack of desire to continue the lesson is to cope with it as you did in the beginning, by running when needed and continuing to teach the stay, showing him that his resistance cannot deter you as he hopes it will. This dog, more than any other, can try your patience and make you lose your temper. This is exactly what he wants and, if he can make you angry enough to break your routine, he will have won out. Continue to work him in the proper way consistently and never allow him to make you lose your temper. If the things he is trying on you are not successful, then he will give them up.

Work your dog for two 15-minute sessions, without distractions, on his complete routine. Follow each session with the usual five-minute break on the 20-foot line, with distractions. In the first session, you should work 15-second stays. With the second session, the stay increases to 25 seconds.

The Fearful Biter and the Aggressive Dog
These dogs should be worked basically like the normal/average dog. Gradually expand the hand signal on the stay. Since it is a threatening gesture to your dog, as you are able to increase the proximity of the hand signal to his face his trust in you will grow, and you will begin to change his attitude favorably. This must be done very gradually.

If corrections are necessary on the stay for these dogs, you may correct them, but the corrections must be followed immediately by verbal praise. Continue to increase the physical praise as your dog is able to accept more. If your dog appears tense on your return, verbally praise him as you draw near. As he becomes more confident, you can omit this verbal praise while returning, and just give physical and verbal praise after you have returned.

Work these dogs for the usual two 15-minute sessions, followed by the two 5-minute breaks. The stays will be 15 seconds during the first session and are increased to 25 seconds for the second session. Work without distractions, but give the breaks with distractions. This ends the fourth day of stays for these dogs.

THE FIFTH DAY

The Normal/Average Dog
Begin working your dog in the usual manner, and then leave him on a stay for 45 seconds. Continue working your dog, and, on the next stay, return after ten seconds. You should now begin to vary the length of the stays. The purpose of this is so that your dog doesn't know how long he is going to have to maintain the stay. He must come to realize that he must stay no matter how long or short the time, and he is released only when you return and praise him.

After working your dog for five minutes on the above routine, you should begin to introduce a small distraction on the stays, which you yourself will provide. After leaving your dog on a stay in the usual manner, instead of standing motionless, facing him from the full six feet away, try taking one or two steps sideways, first to your left and then to your right. You should wind up approximately in the center, still facing your dog. You should then return in the usual manner, take up the leash, and praise him.

On the next stay you should introduce a soft whistle, and then return and praise your dog. Work your dog on a few more automatic sits. Then prepare for another sit-stay. This time you should introduce both distractions from the last stays, moving back and forth and whistling softly, in addition to a new distraction, snapping your fingers lightly a couple of times. Alternate all three distractions on one 45-second stay, and then return in the usual manner and praise your dog.

Many people call their dogs to them by snapping their fingers, whistling, or slapping their hand against their leg. Since these sounds can be made by anyone, your dog must learn to completely ignore them and not respond to these sounds, whether made by his owners or by an utter stranger. The only way you will ever call your dog to you will be by giving the correct verbal command, which will be learned later on. All other inviting sounds must be completely ignored by him. If you have, in the past, called your dog to you by any of these means, you must stop doing so from now on. These sounds will hereafter build in intensity, and be used only as distractions for your dog to ignore.

As you are working your dog, if he should attempt to break the stay, give him a very hard correction and continue building up the distractions until he becomes more reliable and can ignore them with ease. Some day in the future, because of circumstances beyond your control, you may have your dog off the leash and have the need to leave him on a sit-stay. He may be sitting at a curb along a heavily trafficked street, with someone on the other side of the street whistling or snapping his fingers. If the dog breaks and runs into the traffic, he will die. All that holds him there is the memory of your corrections. Make sure your dog remembers that they were very, very hard.

After 15 minutes of this type of workout, give your dog a five-minute break on the long line, with distractions. Then work your dog for another 15 minutes, varying the time of the stays from 10 to 45 seconds so that he does not anticipate a routine. In addition, vary the distractions you used for the first session, building them in frequency as well as intensity. Give your dog his final break on the 20-foot line, with distractions. This ends the fifth day of stays for the normal/average dog.

The Overfriendly Dog and the High-Strung Dog
These dogs should be worked basically like the normal/average dog, the exceptions being that they must be built up much more slowly on the distractions and given abundant praise upon your return. This will show them that they have made the right choice.

Dogs in this category look for any excuse to break their stay. Your distractions provide the ultimate temptation for them. If they do break, you must correct them very firmly. Take your time and build up the distractions very gradually.

Work your dog for two 15-minute sessions, without distractions. Then give him two 5-minute breaks on the 20-foot line, with distractions.

The Aloof Dog
For the sit-stays, the aloof dog can be handled like the normal/average dog. However, you will very likely incur the problem of his consistently breaking the sit-stay. He is trying to convince you that he is confused and doesn't understand, hoping that you'll give up. The truth is that he knows exactly what you want, but is hoping you will not be able to enforce your wishes. He is searching for an area of weakness on your part. Don't let him find it. Correct him repeatedly, as needed; make the corrections very hard and, at the same time, in an emotionless manner.

In all other respects, treat a dog in this category like the normal/average dog. This means two 15-minute sessions without distractions, and two 5-minute breaks on the long line, with distractions.

The Shy/Fearful Dog
This dog should be worked like the overfriendly and high-strung dogs in that you should build up distractions slowly so that corrections are minimal. This dog is usually very willing to please if you only approach him in a consistently gentle manner. Building up distractions too quickly (whistling, finger snapping, etc.), thereby triggering the accompanying corrections, will only serve to break down this dog's confidence and cause a regression in training. He will interpret the corrections as abuse by you, and retreat back into his shell. Nurture this dog slowly. The extra time spent will be well-spent when you consider the reliability of his performance, and, more importantly, the change of attitude in your dog.

Work your dog for two 15-minute sessions, without distractions, followed by two 5-minute breaks on the 20-foot line, with distractions.

The Fearful Biter and the Aggressive Dog
Work these dogs as you would work the overfriendly and the high-strung dogs. This means building up the distractions very, very slowly, so the dog requires minimal corrections. Should you find that your dog requires frequent corrections, then take an extra day or two to build up the distractions (moving left and right, snapping fingers, and whistling) very, very slowly. After this extra time, bring your dog back into the normal routine.

Illus. 67. The sit-stay correction consists of a sharp jerk and release at a distance with the verbal command NO.

Illus. 68. The new command and hand signal for sit and stay given at a distance.

Illus. 69. Training builds a closer bond between you and your dog.

Illus. 70. Take off on your left foot for the heel command.

Illus. 71. Take off on your right foot for the stay command.

Whenever something new is being taught to these types of dogs, they interpret the unknown factors as a threat to themselves. This, in turn, causes a temporary setback in their confidence in you. To help allay this renewed mistrust, you should continue mixing the old, well-learned routine of just praising the dog for his automatic sits, without doing stays for a while, and alternate with the new routine of the stays. This provides the opportunity for praise, and will help your dog to make a less traumatic transition from old to new material.

Two sessions of 15 minutes, plus the two 5-minute breaks on the long line with distractions, will end the fifth day of stays for these dogs.

THE SIXTH DAY

The Normal/Average Dog

With a controlled distraction at one end of the training area, such as someone clanging two pot lids together, or a tied-up dog or cat, enter the training area from the opposite side. Begin working your dog in his heeling routine with right- and left-angle turns, right about-turns, and stops where you just praise him for doing the automatic sit. When he is warmed up and working well, make a stop at least 20 feet from the distraction. Leave your dog by giving the proper STAY command and hand signal. Face him from the six-foot length of the leash, and, after ten seconds, return and praise him. Note that you have not yourself provided any distraction, but are making use of the distraction behind you.

Begin working your dog towards the distraction on everything but stays, moving closer and then away. Continue this until your dog is working very well; then prepare for your next stop, which will be a sit-stay. Whether you had to correct your dog or not, once he is working well leave him on a sit-stay ten feet from the distraction and walk away the full six feet of the leash. Wait ten seconds, and then return and praise him. It would be unfortunate if you would have to correct him from wherever you are when he breaks.

If, after the correction, your dog still does not assume the sit position, give a new command, DREAM, SIT, STAY, and show him the correct hand signal from a distance. If he is still not sitting, give him anther leash correction and continue alternating correction with command until he does sit. It is very important that you realize that you do not have to return to your dog to correct him. It is important that he realize this also.

Begin working your dog again, towards and away from the distraction. At some ten feet from the distraction, give a STAY command and walk out to the full six feet away. Return after 30 seconds, take up the leash, and

praise your dog. When working your dog on the sit-stay, be sure to stand at the side farthest from the distraction, so that your dog is between you and the distraction. Continue working your dog and, after a few automatic sits, leave your dog for another 30-second sit-stay. Return and praise him. Work your dog in his complete routine for the remainder of this first 15-minute session. With the distraction still present, give your dog a five-minute break on the long line in the area opposite the distraction.

After the break, again begin working your dog in his complete routine and, after a warmup, leave him on a sit-stay, about ten feet from the distraction. Make his first one a 30-second stay. Return, take up the leash, and praise your dog. Continue working your dog closer to the distraction until you are only three to four feet away. Come to a stop, leave your dog on a stay for ten seconds, return, take up the leash, and praise your dog. If corrections are necessary, make them very, very hard.

After he has made a few more right about-turns, automatic sits, etc., command your dog to make another stop three or four feet from the distraction. Leave for 20 seconds, return, and praise him. Repeat the routine, moving close and then away, and again leave your dog on a sit-stay three or four feet from the distraction, this time for 30 seconds. Work your dog on sit-stays both close to and far from the distraction. Also, vary the length of time on the stays, with up to a 30-second maximum. Continue working your dog in the above routine for the remainder of this work session. Afterwards, give your dog the usual five-minute break on the 20-foot line, with the distraction still present. This will end the sit-stay for the sixth day for the normal/average dog.

The Overfriendly Dog and the High-Strung Dog

These dogs should be worked like the normal/average dog, except that at no time during the first work session should the dog get closer than 20 feet from the distraction. After the break, which will be on the 20-foot clothesline with the distraction still present, go back for the second session. Then work the dog closer to the distraction, first at ten feet and finally working as close as three or four feet. Remember to correct him hard when it is needed, and give him as much praise as he can handle. Take the final break and end the session for this day.

The Aloof Dog

Handle the aloof dog like the normal/average dog, except correct him very hard when it is needed. Your dog should be between you and the distraction on the stays. He may turn, facing the distraction completely. This is satisfactory as long as he doesn't break the stay. Continue the proper training no matter what your dog does; don't allow him to make you angry or flustered.

Work the usual two 15-minute sessions, with the distraction at one end of the area. Have the distraction remain on the breaks.

The Shy/Fearful Dog

Work the shy/fearful dog like the overfriendly and high-strung dogs. Build up the distraction very slowly, trying to correct as little as possible. When you return, give your dog plenty of praise, making the session a very positive experience for your dog.

Work the two 15-minute sessions, advancing towards the distraction as you did with the overfriendly and high-strung dogs. Give the breaks on the 20-foot line with the distraction still present.

The Fearful Biter and the Aggressive Dog

These dogs should be worked like the normal/average dog with the exceptions that, in the first 15-minute session, you should not get closer than 20 feet to the distraction and the stays should be only ten seconds. In the second session, you should be no closer than 20 feet from the distraction again, but the stays should be 20 seconds long.

If your dog falls into these categories, work him for an extra day or two on the distraction, building him up very slowly until you can take him through the same routine as the normal/average dog for this sixth day. These dogs, especially the aggressive dog, may be able to justify trying to bite you when you try to stop them from going for the distraction. This is why the teaching process must be longer for them. Building them up slowly enables them to accept your corrections; this is preferable to their choosing to contest you with aggression.

Work your dog for the usual two 15-minute sessions and the five-minute breaks on the 20-foot line. After your extra days' work, resume the regular schedule for the seventh day of stays.

THE SEVENTH DAY

The Normal/Average Dog

When you enter the training area, it should be full of assorted distractions such as people, animals, etc. Begin working your dog on heeling and automatic sits until you have gained his full attention. Command him to come to a stop five feet from a distraction. If your dog does not sit immediately, administer a very hard correction. Heel him off, make an about-turn, and come back to within five feet of the same distraction, again making your stop in the same place.

Continue making stops near this distraction until your dog ignores it completely and does a quick automatic sit every time. Only then is he ready for a stay near the distraction. Leave your dog on a stay in the proper fashion. Walk six feet away and stand facing him from the six-foot length of the leash. After 30 seconds, return to his side, take up the leash, and praise him with the words GOOD BOY. Then move off with a new HEEL command.

You should have three or more distractions situated throughout the training area. Approach the next distraction, working your dog on automatic sits. When he is working well, leave him on another stay, again for 30 seconds. Return, take up the leash, and praise him. If your dog breaks any stays, use hard corrections. Approach another distraction and again leave your dog on a stay, this time for a full minute.

For the rest of this session, continue making stops five feet from each distraction, but begin by varying the time of the stays to ten seconds, 30 seconds, or one minute. Continue this routine for the first 15-minute session, and then give him a break on the 20-foot line, not letting him make contact with any of the distractions, and correcting him if he attempts to do so.

After the five-minute break, snap on the leash, snap off the line, make another stop five feet from a distraction, and leave your dog on a stay. With your dog on the stay, lightly snap your fingers, pat your thigh, and whistle softly. After 15 seconds, return, take up the leash, and praise your dog, showing him that he was correct in ignoring the distractions, including the ones you yourself made. Heel him off again, making a stop five feet from a distraction. Give a STAY command and signal. While you are out on the stay, increase the intensity and frequency of your self-made distractions. This time, maintain the stay for 30 seconds. Return, take up the leash, and praise your dog. Continue working this 15-minute session and building up the self-made distractions while working among the external distractions. You should build your dog up to a full minute on the stays; correct him whenever he breaks and start again at a lower level, building him up once again as he is able to handle it.

Never allow your dog to make contact with a distraction when working or when on a break. Should he do so, it will be much harder for you to command his attention afterwards. Continue working your dog as close as five feet from the distractions, varying the time on stays among 10, 30, and 60 seconds. Also vary the intensity and frequency of the self-made distractions, so your dog can never anticipate a set routine. Work the second 15-minute session and then give your dog a final break on the 20-foot line, with the distractions still present. This

Illus. 72. Two owners working two dogs on the sit-stay command from six feet away.

Illus. 73. Down-stays at the six-foot distance.

will end the seventh day on the sit-stay for the normal/average dog.

Your dog will be learning the down command next. In order to obey the down command effectively, he must be able to perform the sit-stay command well. At this point, feel free to work your dog for an extra day or two on the sit-stay. It will make fair dogs good and good dogs even better.

The Overfriendly Dog and the High-Strung Dog

Work these two dogs like the normal/average dog, taking care to build up the distractions that you make very slowly. If forced to correct your dog, use the same distractions, but omit your self-made diversions. After one or two stays without your own distractions, you may reintroduce them, building your dog up slowly again. Build these dogs to the reliable level described for the normal/average dog. Take an extra day or two on the stays to make them more secure, if needed, in preparation for the down command to follow.

The Aloof Dog

Work this dog like the normal/average dog, consistently correcting him hard when needed. If your dog slows down to look at a distraction behind him, correct him by breaking into a run for a few yards. Make sure your dog is reliable on the stays before moving on to the more difficult down command that follows.

The Shy/Fearful Dog

Work this dog like the normal/average dog, but build him up slowly and give him ample praise when it is justified.

The Fearful Biter and the Aggressive Dog

Work these dogs like the normal/average dog, with the exception that the first two stays will be no closer than 20 feet from the distraction. Build up your dog until he can get as close as five feet and is performing on the level of the normal/average dog. It is very important that these dogs be worked at the level described for the normal/average dog before you attempt to teach the down command, which follows. When leaving him on the stays, be sure that your dog is between you and the distraction so that, in case he breaks, he cannot make physical contact with it.

When your dog can reliably sit and stay five feet from a distraction (Illus. 72–78), then he will be ready to learn the hardest command of all for you and for him: the down command.

Fifth "Week": The Down Command (Illus. 79–94)

The command DOWN will be a specific command that will mean to your dog that you want him to lie down prone on the ground (Illus. 79). It will be used in conjunction with the command STAY, and the down-stay will be the most effective way of controlling your dog in times of maximum excitement and possible danger. Because the down-stay is comfortable, your dog can hold this position for a very long time.

The command DOWN will be the most difficult of all for your dog to learn. The reason for this is that dogs consider the act of lying down as complete submission to an opponent. In a fight between dogs, the loser can often save himself further injury or death by lying down and submitting to his opponent. Usually, a severe beating must be administered by an opponent to make the losing dog lie down in this way. Therefore, when you command your dog to lie down, you are asking much more from him than may seem obvious.

Special techniques will be used to teach the dog the down command. The authors have found these techniques to be most effective and least punitive from the dog's point of view. When you tell your dog DOWN, this will mean to him that you want him to lie down immediately at your command. To avoid any possible confusion in his mind, and to keep things simplest for him, say DOWN only when you want your dog to lie down, and not when you want him to get off a couch or stop jumping on someone. For all these other transgressions, use the word NO. In this way, the command DOWN will not be a reprimand, but just another command that will not be as offensive to him or as hard to take from you.

Teaching the DOWN command will be accomplished in two distinct phases. The first part will consist of physically placing him in the down position, while at the same time saying the dog's name and DOWN. The second phase will consist of correcting the dog for not lying down, and proving to him that you can not only correct him if he refuses to lie down, but that you can physically knock him to the ground each time he refuses to obey your down command.

There are many diverse methods for teaching a dog to lie down. They vary among professional dog trainers. Most of these methods consist of the basic technique of applying a downward pressure on the leash with either the trainer's hand or foot, and gradually increasing the pressure as the command DOWN is given, until the pressure causes the struggling dog finally to submit and lie down. The amount of punishment that some dogs take as they resist the downward pressure employed with this method is excessive beyond need and, with very stubborn dogs, can greatly intensify. It is harder to teach some dogs the down command than others, but the amount of punishment they must receive when learning it can be greatly minimized by using the more positive method that follows.

Since we are fighting the dog's natural tendency to resist us, we want the teaching method as pleasant as possible for him. There is no way a dog can enjoy or even passively tolerate having someone step on his leash or apply manual pressure to slowly pull him to the ground. However, contrast this with our method, which will consist of gently, with your left hand on his back and your right hand holding his front paws, placing him in the down position and praising him lavishly as soon as he is lying down. It will take you about five days to teach your dog this placing process, so your dog will have all this time to learn what DOWN means before ever being corrected for not lying down. When he finally is corrected, he will be given very strong corrections in a downward direction, in a special way that will knock him off his feet, causing him to lie down. In the other methods, after the dog is choked for ten or 15 minutes in the down position, the corrections are made in an upward direction each time the dog refuses to lie down when commanded.

At this time, you may ask yourself, "Isn't this exactly like a sit correction? Won't this make my dog think I want him to sit, thereby confusing him?" The answer is "Yes," which is precisely why we are correcting him in a downward direction. He will have a clear idea as to what is expected of him. We will now proceed with the actual teaching of the down command.

THE FIRST DAY

The Normal/Average Dog
Enter the training area with your dog. Make sure there are no distractions in the area. Begin working your dog on the entire routine, including automatic sits, sit-stays, heeling, etc. When he is warmed up and working well, come to a stop.

As soon as he does his automatic sit, place him down in the following manner. With the leash held entirely in your right hand, place your left hand on his head as if to praise him. Drop the leash to the ground from your right hand (Illus. 80); drop it in front of you, where you can easily step on it or grab it if the need arises. Run your left hand down your dog's neck; stop in the middle of his back, and place the open palm of your hand on his back.

Then bend forward and, with your right hand, reach under his front legs. Reach with your right hand twisted forward, knuckles down, palm upward, thumb pointed in the direction the dog is facing. With your right hand, reach under the foot closest to you and grab the second foot, which is the dog's left front foot (Illus. 81).

Next, lift the front legs slightly and push forward while, at the same time, exerting downward pressure on the dog's back with your left hand (Illus. 82). As your dog is reaching the down position, speak the command, DREAM, DOWN. The emphasis is on the word DOWN, which should be much louder and drawn out than the word that precedes it. As soon as your dog is down, lavishly praise him, giving as much praise as he can handle (Illus. 83). Then grab the leash near his neck with your right hand and move off with a new HEEL command, taking up the proper hand grip and straightening out the leash as you walk.

Place your dog down on a soft surface, such as the living-room rug or a soft lawn. Do not send him crashing down on a hard cement surface, which will only serve to build up his resistance and apprehension. Also, be sure to move in quickly and securely. Don't allow your dog to anticipate your moves and wiggle away from you in resistance.

Dogs are great natural students of body language. They are very aware of the way other animals and people move. If you want your dog to trust you and be confident in what you are doing, you must move smoothly and surely into each maneuver and so impart to your dog the belief that you are indeed quite confident and capable. To accomplish this, you must be thoroughly familiar with the movements required of you as you place your dog down. Study Illus. 79–83 carefully and try to visualize the specific movements before actually applying the techniques to your dog.

Use the placement method as described above on all breeds, with the exception of some of the very small toy breeds. The method for those dogs will be modified slightly. Instead of reaching in with your right hand and grabbing a leg, since the dog is so small you will just have room enough to reach in with one or two fingers behind his front legs. Then push forward as you use your left hand to push down on his back, sweeping him to the ground, where you immediately praise him.

Continue working your dog on heeling, do a sit-stay or two, and then, as you're heeling him, come to a stop. As he sits, move in quickly and place him down. Remember to say the word DOWN louder than your dog's name. Also, make the command long and drawn out: DOOWWWN!

It is important to note that your dog should not be

Illus. 74. Two dogs starting out at the heel position. The stay command is being given.

Illus. 75. Note that the leash is taken up at different lengths for the two different-size dogs.

Illus. 76. Two small dogs can be worked together on the left side.

Illus. 77. The equipment for tiny dogs can consist of a strap collar or a nylon choke and leash.

placed down repeatedly, again and again, but, instead, the routine should be varied so that he cannot predict any regular order to your routine. Never do two downs in a row; instead, always add a sit, and then a sit-stay or some heeling with automatic sits before doing another down. Work your dog on this routine throughout the first 15-minute session; then give him his usual break on the 20-foot clothesline, with distractions. After the break, bring him back for an exact repetition of the first 15-minute session, including review of all his other work. After the second session, give him his final break and leave the area, ending the first day's session on the down.

The Overfriendly Dog and the High-Strung Dog

Work these dogs like the normal/average dog. After they have been placed down one or two times, these dogs will anticipate what you are doing and will quickly move to block your initial grab for them. Your best counter for this is to mix up the routine so they never know when you are going to do the down command, and to move in on them very quickly when you do place them down. These dogs also may present a problem by defecating or urinating on the leash, either purposely or accidentally, after they are placed down. They may roll over on their backs and tangle the leash around one or both of their front paws. These dogs are attempting to put a stop to your routine. To counteract this, with your right hand simply grab the leash near the dog's neck, where it meets his collar (Illus. 84), and, giving a new HEEL command, walk away as you take up the leash with the proper hand grip.

Another way your dog may protest this routine is by holding on to your right hand with his mouth. It is his way of telling you he doesn't like what you are doing and would like you to stop. He is hoping, once again, to break up your routine by getting you excited. The best way to stop this is simply to remove your right hand a split second before he touches the ground. Swing it out and down near your right hip, leaving him nothing to grab. If you practise this maneuver a few times, you will be able to take your dog down, and have your right hand by your side by the time he hits the ground.

The last form of protest that these dogs may attempt is to roll over completely on their backs and paw the air. Rolling over on their backs, after being placed down in the beginning, is okay, and you should still praise your dog for lying down. But if he rolls over in a wild, frantic manner, you must stop this immediately by grabbing the leash near his neck and quickly moving off with a new HEEL command.

Vary the routine and work these dogs for the usual two 15-minute sessions, without distractions; also you should give them the usual two breaks on the 20-foot line, with distractions.

The Aloof Dog

Work the aloof dog as you would the normal/average dog. He may renew his resistance to walking with you. This should be counteracted by your running when you start to heel him. He may also try to place your right hand in his mouth as you place him down. You should remove your right hand quickly, before your dog hits the ground, so that it is out of his way and unable to provide the interruption in routine that he is hoping for.

Work your dog for two 15-minute sessions, without distractions. Give him his two 5-minute breaks on the 20-foot line, with distractions.

The Shy/Fearful Dog

The shy/fearful dog should be worked like the normal/average dog, except that he should be prepared for the down placement, rather than directly placing him down. To prepare your dog for the down, leave him on a sit-stay. After a few seconds, return to his side. Stroke his side and legs, hesitate, and then praise him. Make the next few stops just sit-stays, where you will return and touch him lightly, hesitating and then praising him. After about six or seven of these touching maneuvers, your dog will be ready to be placed down gently. Place him like you did the normal/average dog, and give him abundant praise once he is down.

Work this dog for the usual two 15-minute sessions, without distractions, along with the two 5-minute breaks on the 20-foot line, with distractions.

The Fearful Biter and the Aggressive Dog

Build these dogs up gradually, using preliminary touching before placing them down. As you start to place these dogs down, it is sometimes helpful if you praise them verbally before they touch the ground. This gets them over a worrisome moment. In all other ways, work these dogs exactly as you did the normal/average dog.

The two work sessions will be 15 minutes, without distractions; there will be two 5-minute breaks on the 20-foot line, with distractions.

THE SECOND DAY

All Dogs

Work each of these dogs as they were worked on the first day of the down placement. Concentrate on building up the time on sit-stays to a minute and a half. Throughout the entire routine, continue to place them down, alternating commands so as not to become predictable.

Work the two 15-minute sessions without distractions.

Give the five-minute breaks on the 20-foot line, with distractions.

THE THIRD DAY

All Dogs
Work each of these dogs as they were worked on the first and second days of the down placement. By now, you should be encountering less resistance as you place them down.

If, after a few days, you find your dog almost lying down on your command, steps must be taken to prevent him from doing so at this time. You should continue to place him down, with your left hand on his back and your right hand sweeping his front legs forward, not allowing him to lie down on his own at this time. It is very important, and cannot be emphasized enough, that your dog must not be allowed to lie down on your command without being properly placed down by you. If your dog were allowed to lie down at this point, you would never, in the future, have as reliable and immediate a down response as will be achieved by following the methods exactly as prescribed.

Work your dog for his usual two 15-minute sessions, without distractions, and have two 5-minute breaks on the 20-foot line, with distractions.

THE FOURTH DAY

All Dogs
Work each of these dogs as they were worked on the previous days of the down placement. Work your dog for the usual two 15-minute sessions, without distractions, and two 5-minute breaks on the 20-foot line, with distractions present.

THE FIFTH DAY

All Dogs
For most dogs, this fifth day will probably be the last day you will have to place them down. Work each of these dogs as you did on the previous days. By this time, your dog must allow himself to be placed down freely and easily by you. He should be very familiar with what you are doing, and should not be trying to contest it at all. If there remains any resistance on your dog's part to being placed down by you, then do *not* at this time go on to the sixth day's training routine. Instead, continue to place your dog on the down for an extra day or two, until he accepts the down freely.

Work your dog for the usual two 15-minute sessions, without distractions. Also give him the two 5-minute breaks on the 20-foot line, with distractions. This will end the fifth day of the down for your dog.

THE SIXTH DAY

This will be a memorable day for your dog. For the past five days you have been teaching him what the word DOWN means by physically placing him down. Now you can assume that he knows what the word DOWN means and what is expected of him when given the command. From this point on, the teaching process ceases. You will never again place him down. You must just correct him every time he does not lie down at your command. These corrections will be more powerful and different than any he has received previously.

It is very important, for this day's training session, that the dog be worked in an area completely free of distractions. If you don't have a suitable outside area, then the next best place to work your dog would be in a quiet room in the house. If you choose to work your dog inside, a smooth, hard slippery surface will make things easier for both you and your dog.

The Normal/Average Dog
Enter the training area and begin working your dog in his complete routine. When he is warmed up and working well, come to a stop and, as he does his automatic sit, turn to your left so that you are facing your dog and almost in front of him. Holding the leash slack with both hands, bend forward slightly and give the command by saying the dog's name and DOWN (Illus. 85). Remain motionless for four seconds. There must be no tension whatsoever on the leash when you give the command. If the dog does not lie down, which is most often the case, after four seconds you should correct him as follows. With both hands on the leash, slowly move your hands towards the dog, starting approximately a foot and a half from the dog's neck (Illus. 86) (this varies with the size of the dog, smaller ones requiring less distance and larger ones requiring more); then sharply move your hands in a downward, forceful, silent correction (Illus. 87). This correction should be angled slightly to your left, which is also the dog's right front.

One such smooth, powerful correction, if properly administered, should knock your dog to the ground in the down position (Illus. 88). As soon as your dog is in the down position, immediately step back to heel position and praise him lavishly (Illus. 89). The reason why the correction is not directly in front of the dog is that he would be able to brace himself against it with both legs. But, delivered from the side, the force of the correction is exerted almost entirely on his right front foot, easily knocking him down.

Illus. 78. Holding small dogs in your arms excessively can make them insecure and cause injuries if you drop them.

Illus. 79. The down command.

Illus. 80. Return to heel position (do not take up the leash), left hand on your dog's back as you bend down. Never drop the leash completely when outside.

Illus. 81. Reach behind your dog's right-front leg to grab his left-front leg. Lift his legs up and forward.

It is important that you study Illus. 86 and 87 very carefully so that you may perform this maneuver correctly. If your dog is very big, or you have not done the correction properly, or, for any reason, you were not able to knock him to the ground with your first correction, then, after four seconds, give him a new command by saying his name and the word DOWN and, four seconds later, a new, more powerful, silent correction, if he doesn't obey. But if he *does* go down, quickly step back to the heel position and praise him, moving off with a new HEEL command.

If your dog still did not lie down for you after the second correction, then continue alternating commands with corrections until you either knock him down or have him give in and lie down for you. It doesn't matter whether you have to knock your dog down or he lies down by himself, your dog should always get praised once he is in the down position. Make two more stops, where you just praise the dog for doing the automatic sit. Then, on the third sit, turn and face your dog, bowing forward slightly, and again give the DOWN command. After the four-second wait, if he has not lain down, do the down correction, get back to the heel position, and immediately praise him, moving off with a new HEEL command. Continue working your dog, alternating among stays, automatic sits, and downs until your dog is lying down at your DOWN command every time you give it.

Some dogs require only one or two down corrections before they will give in and lie down at your command. Others may require as many as ten or more corrections. Occasionally, in rare instances, some dogs will require as many as 20 or 30 of these corrections before they will give in and lie down. No matter how many corrections your particular dog requires, whether it be two or 30, make sure that you provide them. You must have complete confidence in what you are doing and persevere until the dog lies down. There is no doubt that your dog has been more than adequately prepared for these corrections, because you have placed him down for the previous five days.

Disregard the normal 15-minute time limit for this particular phase. You must continue the correction until the dog lies down; it is the only possible ending for this training session. Even though your dog gives in and lies down for you the first time, this is not the time to stop. He still may require more corrections. After you have four successive downs in a row, you can be confident that he has given in almost 100 percent and now deserves a break. The usual break on the 20-foot line, with no distractions present, should be given after the first training session.

Begin the second session by warming your dog up with a couple of automatic sits. On the third stop, turn to your left, facing your dog, and give the DOWN command. If he lies down, step back to the heel position and praise him. If he chooses not to, let your correction leave no doubt that he has definitely made the wrong choice. Whether he lies down himself or is knocked down by your corrections, once he is down you should step back to the heel position and praise him.

Continue working your dog, and again mix up the routine, doing a stay, an automatic sit, and then a down. Occasionally, some dogs will renew their resistance during this second session. If this is the case with your dog, just continue to correct him in the usual manner until he lies down again. This day's training session must end only one way, with your dog lying down. The 15-minute time limit again will not apply, and you should not end this second session until you have gotten four successive downs from him. If you get the four downs in a row quickly, then you may end this second session after a few minutes. The usual five-minute break, without distractions, will end this day's training session.

Let's take a moment and review what you have done today, from your dog's point of view. You have spent five days teaching him, in a very pleasant way, what the command DOWN meant. Two or three days would have been enough for almost any dog, but you gave five full days with two sessions each day. You left no doubt what the word DOWN means. For a dog, knowing something does not mean he will always do it. Sometimes it takes a little more; sometimes he needs to know that you can always make him do what you want. After you taught him what DOWN meant, you then told him to lie down and, when he didn't, showed him that you were capable of knocking him to the ground. You maintained consistency in that, every time he refused to comply, you proved your capabilities by again knocking him down. No matter how he got there, once he was down he always was praised.

After today's training session your dog must have a new world of respect for you and your capabilities. Your dog will never forget what happened today, and his response to your DOWN commands in the future will be faster and better than you ever thought possible.

Note: From this day forward, be certain that you never use the word DOWN for anything other than to instruct your dog to lie down. All other negative behavior, such as jumping on people or on furniture, will be handled with one word: NO.

The Overfriendly Dog and The High-Strung Dog
These dogs should be worked like the normal/average dog, except that when they are lying down, you should

104

give only a controlled amount of praise. If they lie down but then jump right up, this is okay for now, because the down is just a down and not a down-stay yet. Work these dogs for the two sessions with no distractions, and take the two 5-minute breaks on the 20-foot line, also without distractions.

The Aloof Dog

The aloof dog is worked like the normal/average dog and may require many corrections. Make as many corrections as it takes in this day's training session until the dog lies down. Extremely hard corrections are needed for this dog. Work the two sessions, without distractions, and two 5-minute breaks on the 20-foot line, also without distractions.

The Shy/Fearful Dog

Work the shy/fearful dog like the normal/average dog, giving him bountiful praise every time he lies down or is knocked down. Work this dog for two sessions, without distractions, and two 5-minute breaks on the long line, also without distractions.

The Fearful Biter and the Aggressive Dog

These dogs should once again be tied to the stakes with the 12-foot line, as was described on the first day of heeling for them. It is very important that you do not attempt what follows without first taking this precaution. It is quite certain that at this stage of training your dog can take physical corrections from you without thinking of biting you; however, because of the newness of today's routine, the possibility exists that some dogs might make a mistake. So, play it safe and begin with the dog tied to the stake with the 12-foot safety line, in any case.

Begin heeling your dog in a counterclockwise circle around the stake or tree. Work him on a couple of stops with just automatic sits, and then work him on a sit-stay, and then a couple of additional automatic sits. Make a right turn and come to a stop with the safety line taut. You and your dog should be facing away from the stake. Give a STAY command and leave, only going two feet from him; then turn and face him.

At this point your dog should not be able to reach you or make physical contact with you. He should be restrained by the safety line. Give your dog the command by saying his name and DOWN as you face him from two feet away, bowing forward slightly. If your dog lies down, verbally praise him and move off with a new HEEL command, continuing to walk around the stake in a counterclockwise circle. If, after four seconds, he does not lie down, immediately correct him in the following manner: Tightly holding the leash with both your hands together, slowly move towards the dog to create slack in the leash. Then silently jerk in the downward direction, to your left side, with one powerful thrust. This correction should be so forceful that it immediately compels your dog to lie down. If, for any reason, he is still not lying down, repeat the command and, after four seconds, provide a new correction. If necessary, continue alternating correction with command until the dog lies down. No matter how many corrections it takes, once he is down, verbally praise him and move on with a new HEEL command, continuing to walk around the stake in a counterclockwise circle.

If your dog should misjudge your intentions and attempt to bite you as you are correcting him for the down, he will be stopped by the safety line after moving an inch or two. After his aggression has ceased, tell him to SIT and STAY and, stepping back two feet, bow forward and again give the DOWN command.

Repeat the procedure of correcting your dog in this manner every time he attempts to bite you, and immediately move on to a new DOWN command and corrections. As soon as he is down, verbally praise him and heel him off, continuing in a counterclockwise circle around the stake. Continue by making a couple of stops with just automatic sits; and again turning to the right, stopping, facing away from the stake, give the STAY command and leave your dog. Then turn and face him from two feet away. Give the DOWN command and if, after four seconds, he does not respond, again correct him in the downward direction. If he lies down, praise him; if not, continue alternating every four seconds between correction and command until you win out. Then move off in a counterclockwise direction with a new HEEL command.

When you get four successful downs in a row, without any corrections being needed, you may end the first part of the day's training with the usual break. The break will be in the same distraction-free area, with the 20-foot line dragging. After the break, bring your dog back to the safety line and begin heeling him counterclockwise around the stake as before. After a couple of stops with just automatic sits, again come to a stop with both of you facing outside of the circle. Give the STAY command. Turn facing him from two feet away and give the DOWN command. After four seconds, if he lies down, praise him, and move off with a new HEEL command.

After two more successful downs you can unsnap the safety line and begin working him exactly as before, including around the circle to make it look the same to him. Continue working him as before, mixing automatic sits, sit-stays, and downs for another five minutes. Then give him the usual five-minute break in the same

Illus. 82. Lift your dog up, forward, and down while maintaining pressure on his back.

Illus. 83. The dog in the down position, being praised.

distraction-free area, on the 20-foot line, and end this session for today. You should never again need a safety line on your dog.

THE SEVENTH DAY

The Normal/Average Dog

Enter the training area with your dog. Warm him up with the usual routine of heeling, automatic sits, and an occasional stay. Then come to a stop and, as soon as he sits, bow forward slightly and give your dog the DOWN command. Needless to say, if he failed to lie down after four seconds, you would correct him in the usual manner.

Work your dog on a few automatic sits and then come to a stop. Give your dog the DOWN command. As soon as he is down, give him an additional STAY command, which will consist of the word STAY and your open hand in front of his face (Illus. 90). Leave him by stepping out only two steps, and then turn and face him. Then immediately return to his side, praise him, and move off with a new HEEL command.

At the next stop, leave your dog on a short 15-second sit-stay, return, praise him, and move on with a new HEEL command. Next, come to a stop and, when he sits, command him by calling his name and DOWN; then, as soon as he complies, give the command word and signal: STAY. Again, leave some two feet from him and turn facing him, this time for ten seconds. Return and praise your dog.

If your dog has a tendency to sit up as you return to praise him, return slowly and hesitate three or four seconds before praising him. This will help to keep him there as he waits for the praise.

Continue working your dog on the entire heeling routine. Then come to a stop and command your dog by calling his name, and then DOWN and STAY. This time walk a full six feet away before turning to face him. If he breaks at this point by getting up, you must correct him by applying a downward horizontal jerk, together with the word NO (Illus. 91). This should occur as he is getting up. Then, if he does not lie down, give a new command by saying his name and DOWN and, once he is down, add the command STAY as you show him the palm of your hand from the full six feet away.

After ten seconds, return to your dog's side, praise him, and move on with a new HEEL command. Vary the work for a few minutes until you again come to a stop and do another down-stay from the entire six-foot length of the leash, this time for 20 seconds (Illus. 92–94). Return to his side, praise him, and heel him near to where the 20-foot line is lying on the ground. Give him

his usual break on the 20-foot line at this time. There will be no distractions for the work session or the breaks.

For the second training session, work all the obedience commands, including the down-stays, so that there is no predictable pattern to them. Vary the length of time of the down-stays from 15 to 30 seconds for this entire session.

Occasionally, after learning the DOWN command, a dog will start lying down by himself as, for example, on a sit-stay. This usually means that you are doing too many downs or giving the DOWN command too often to your dog. If this should occur with your dog, the first and best correction would be to prevent it from happening at all by doing very few downs for a while; this shows him that he is not going to lie down very frequently, but only occasionally. The other correction takes place when he is on a sit-stay and decides to lie down without command. Watch closely as he starts to move towards the ground. Take up the slack in the leash, holding it in your left hand, level with your chest. With an upward swing, catch the leash in the palm of your right hand and exert an upward tension, making it difficult for your dog to lie down. Then say your dog's name and SIT and STAY, showing him the palm of your hand. If your dog should make it to the down position before you can exert an upward tension on the leash, you must return to him, lift him up by the collar (not the leash) back into the sit position, repeat his name and the commands SIT and STAY, and leave for a second time. It is, of course, preferable to catch him before he lies down.

Never jerk your dog if he starts to lie down by himself. This will just make him lie down. Vary the work and, after 15 minutes, end the session with the usual five-minute break. Both work sessions and breaks should have to distractions present.

The Overfriendly Dog and the High-Strung Dog

Work these dogs as you would the normal/average dog. Work very gradually with them on the down-stays.

The Aloof Dog

Work the aloof dog as you would the normal/average dog, remembering to correct him very hard if he renews any of his resistance.

The Shy/Fearful Dog

Work the shy/fearful dog as you would the normal/average dog. This dog has a tendency to lie down too much, which may take the form of lying down while on a sit-stay or an automatic sit. The previous remedies apply here, such as working very few downs, demonstrating to the dog that the down command will not be used frequently. As he realizes this, his confidence will return and he will remain sitting up. If, while on a sit-stay, he attempts to lie down by himself, exert the upward tension on the leash with your right hand, thereby preventing him from doing so. While holding him up, just verbally praising him very softly with the words GOOD BOY, JUST RELAX will help to give him confidence and keep him up.

If your dog starts to lie down automatically each time you stop, the way to work him out of this problem is, first, to do very few, or no, downs for a while, and second, make a few stops of a half-second duration. These stops will be so short that he barely has time to sit before you walk off again. This quick routine will build up his confidence, as well as make it impossible for him to lie down.

The Fearful Biter and the Aggressive Dog
These dogs should be worked as you would the normal/average dog. If a fearful/biter lies down too often, handle him as you did the dogs in the previous sections.

Sixth "Week": The Recall
(Illus. 95–98 and 103)

Everyone wants his dog to come to him when called. There are two primary ways to help ensure that your dog will come. First, you must convince your dog that you can always make him come when you call him. Then, you must make coming to you an extremely pleasant thing for your dog by praising him lavishly each time he does so. This means that calling your dog to you to reprimand him or punish him for something he has done just then, or previously, is a definite mistake. We cannot emphasize this enough: If your dog learns that coming to you is going to mean punishment for him, then he is not going to be thrilled with the prospect of coming to you. Remember the way dogs learn. Those experiences that bring unpleasant results are discontinued; those that bring pleasant results are continued. Make sure your dog has a pleasant association in mind when you call him.

THE FIRST DAY
The Normal/Average Dog
Enter the training area with your dog on the leash and begin working him on the entire obedience routine in a distraction-free area. The routine should consist of the entire heeling procedure, including all appropriate turns and stops, an occasional sit-stay, an occasional down-stay. After some three or four minutes, when your dog is warmed up and working well, leave him on a sit-stay and, as usual, stand facing him from the six-foot length of the leash. You should now call your dog to come to you in the following manner: As you are standing facing your dog, without moving transfer the leash to your left hand (Illus. 95). With your right hand, reach out towards your dog and slowly draw your hand back to your chest as you give the verbal command by saying the dog's name and COME (Illus. 96). The emphasis should be on the command word COME.

Your dog will have only one of two reactions to this new command. The first and most desirable reaction will be that he comes to you. Without pulling on the leash, take it up, hand over hand and, as he comes close to you, give the command SIT. As soon as he sits in front of you, quickly move to the heel position and praise him. Notice that he was not praised just for coming to you, but only after he came and then sat. The recall is such a vital command that it is important to add the sit as an ending. Your dog will strive to give you more than just a recall, so his concentrating on the sit will help him to do a better recall.

The other reaction your dog may have will be not to come, but to remain either sitting or standing just looking at you. If this is the case with your dog, then simply show him that you can make him follow the command by taking up the leash hand over hand and "reeling" him in and, as he draws close to you, giving the command SIT. As soon as he is sitting, smoothly step to the heel position at his side and praise him.

Although you want your dog to sit in front of you after he comes to you, this is one time when you must *not* correct him if he does not sit or refuses your SIT command as he comes close to you. If coming to you means that he is going to get jerked with a correction, then he would consider it an unpleasant thing. Therefore, once your dog is in front of you, if he refuses the SIT command push on his rear end and place him on a sit. Then lavishly praise him, thus making this a pleasant experience for him.

Begin working your dog again. Come to a stop and leave him on a down-stay. After a minute, return to him, take up the leash, and praise him. Continue heeling your dog, and do a sit-stay in which you just return to him and praise him. On your next stop, leave him on a sit-stay and, after ten seconds, call him to you. Remember, the emphasis is on the command word COME. Say the dog's name and then emphasize the word COME. Once you sit him in front of you, move to the heel position at his side and praise him, moving off with a new HEEL command.

It is important to note at this time that no recalls will be made for now from the down position, but will only

Illus. 84. The dog in the down position, fouling the leash. When this occurs, grab the leash near his neck and walk away. The leash will come free as you walk; then take it up properly.

Illus. 85. Command your dog by saying his name and DOWN from this position.

be done while your dog is on the sit-stay. The reason you will not call your dog to you from the down-stay at this time is that you want your dog to know that the down-stay should be made in a consistent manner. To ensure this, you will show your dog that he will not be asked to break the down-stay to come to you from this position.

Continue working your dog on the entire routine of heeling, sit-stays, down-stays, and recalls from the sit-stay for the remainder of this first 15-minute training session. Remember, just as with the down, recalls should not be repeated over and over, but the work should always be varied so your dog will not be able to anticipate any predictable pattern in your routine. Teaching a dog the recall is teaching him to break the stay. If the recall is overdone, then his reliability on the stay will be adversely affected. Always give your dog a varied work routine.

Give your dog a five-minute break on the 20-foot line, with distractions present. At the end of the break, stand on the clothesline he is dragging and call him to you the same way as before, by saying his name and COME. Whether he comes or not, "reel" him in. Once he is sitting in front of you, move to the heel position and praise him lavishly. With one quick motion, snap on the leash, snap off the clothesline, and begin working your dog on the entire obedience routine, varying the work among sit-stays, down-stays, and recalls. At the end of this work period, give your dog another five-minute break on the 20-foot line. This will end the session for this day. It is extremely important that once the training session is over neither you nor anyone else should ever call the dog unless you are in the position to "reel" him in, thereby enforcing your command. The misuse of this command would be counterproductive and actually tend to undo the day's training.

The Overfriendly Dog and the High-Strung Dog
Work these dogs like the normal/average dog, but also increase the down-stay to a full minute, varying the work among the sit-stays, down-stays, and recalls. These dogs will need a controlled amount of praise; otherwise, they will take advantage of you and jump all over you. This may mean that, once your dog is sitting in front of you, your praise will be verbal only, to keep things better under control. Gradually, as your dog can accept more praise, you will be able to increase the amount of praise.

If these dogs are too excitable once they reach you, and jump exuberantly before you can give them the SIT command, try giving the SIT command while they are still approaching you and are a few feet away. This will start them concentrating on sitting, rather than jumping once they have arrived in front of you. If they attempt to run right past you, maintain close control on the leash, exerting a slight tension, and steer them directly in front of you. There you should then command them to SIT, with your own body maintaining a very still and erect posture. Remember, never correct your dog for not sitting on the recall. Place him, if necessary. Your dog is being praised for coming to you, which he already has done. The sit is to finalize and make his recall even more secure.

Work your dog for the usual two 15-minute sessions, without distractions, with the usual two 5-minute breaks on the 20-foot line, with distractions. Remember to conclude each break by calling your dog to you and then "reeling" him in on the long line.

The Aloof Dog
Work the aloof dog like the normal/average dog. You most likely will have to reel in this dog for a while, since he generally is not interested in complying with your wishes (Illus. 97). Increase the down-stays to a full minute, and vary the work routine among sit-stays, down-stays, and recalls.

Work the two 15-minute sessions without distractions. Give the five-minute breaks on the 20-foot line, with distractions, remembering to end each with a recall.

The Shy/Fearful Dog
Work the shy/fearful dog as you would the normal/average dog, with the exception that, when you give the recall command, you should bend low and praise your dog softly as he moves towards you. You should bend low whether you have to "reel" him in or he comes in himself. As he draws near to you, stand up straight and give the command SIT (Illus. 98). Bending low will make you less imposing and will tend to make your dog come to you more freely. Standing up, once he is near, will have the opposite effect and make him sit. Remember, if these dogs have been called and then reprimanded in the past, you will have to overcome their fear of coming to you by your proper handling and by consistency in working the recall as described above. These dogs should always be lavishly praised after the recall.

Work your dog for two 15-minute sessions, without distractions, and give him two 5-minute breaks on the 20-foot line, with distractions. End each break by doing a recall on the long line.

The Fearful Biter and the Aggressive Dog
Work these dogs as you would the normal/average dog, with down-stays, sit-stays, and recalls. When giving the recall command, praise these dogs as they walk towards you. Then give the SIT command and, whether you

have to place them or they sit by themselves, lavishly praise them once you have returned to heel position.

Work these dogs for two 15-minute sessions, without distractions, and give them two 5-minute breaks on the 20-foot line, with distractions. Finish the breaks by doing a final recall on the long line.

THE SECOND DAY

All Dogs
All the dogs should be worked just as they were on the first day of the recall. This means no distractions for the work sessions. However, you should increase the down-stays to a minute and a half.

THE THIRD DAY

All Dogs
Work all the dogs just as on the previous day, with the exception that you should increase the time on the down-stays to two minutes. Also, there should be a distraction at one end of the area throughout the training sessions and breaks.

THE FOURTH DAY

All Dogs
All these dogs should be worked as on the previous days, the exception being that you will provide multiple distractions throughout the area on both the work sessions and the breaks. The sit-stays will remain at 1½ minutes and the down-stays will be increased to 2½ minutes.

THE FIFTH DAY

All Dogs
All dogs should be worked as for the previous days. Increase the down-stays to three full minutes, with multiple distractions.

THE SIXTH DAY

All Dogs
On this day, take your dog out of the area to a shopping center or some other heavily trafficked place where many new distractions can be provided for him. Work him on all the commands near people, cars, shopping carts, stairs, and every distraction that you and he confront. Work him, praise him, and work him more, as both of you conquer each new distraction. When problems are encountered with a particular distraction, continue to work him near it and you and he will soon conquer it.

THE SEVENTH DAY

All Dogs
Enter the training area with your dog on the leash. Begin heeling him and leave him on a sit-stay. Take a good look at him. You and he have come a long way. Remember six weeks ago when you started working him? Remember that first day and how wild and difficult it was for both of you? Now he sits there attentively watching you. In six short weeks, you've created a bond of respect and understanding between you and your dog that has increased with every passing day. You are to be congratulated, but you must also understand one thing: You've only just begun training your dog! In six short weeks you've travelled a long way, but how far can you both go in six weeks or six months more? Dogs differ from all other animals because of their great desire to please us. The authors of this book hope that you will continue to work your dog so that you both can realize your full potential.

Off-Leash Work

Illus. 99–104 and 106 and 107 show Bill and Daisy engaged in advanced off-leash work involving the same basic commands that have just been dicussed. There is specific intensive training required to reach this level of obedience.

Illus. 86. Begin correcting your dog with your hands close to his face, for maximum downward thrust.

Illus. 87. The downward impact will knock the dog to the ground.

Illus. 88. The dog in the down position.

Illus. 89. The dog in the down position at heel.

Adult Problems

Barking

Barking is a natural way for a dog to articulate many feelings. Most people want their dog to give warning barks, as, for example, when people come to call or when the mailman comes to deliver mail or packages. This is because the dog owner may be doing laundry in the basement, listening to a loud radio or TV, taking a shower, gardening in the backyard, or doing any number of other things that would keep him or her from hearing the doorbell.

Another more obvious reason dog owners want their dogs to bark is to warn threatening intruders not to come any closer. Burglars are often discouraged by the warning sound of a barking dog.

Many dogs naturally learn to protect the household and yard. Some dogs do not have this propensity and would invite the burglar in for coffee and cake if they could. All people are potential pals and playmates for these types of dog. Many people make quite an effort to encourage their less-verbal dogs to bark at noises by praising the barking at any time and encouraging the behavior at specific times.

Dogs bark for many reasons. They bark when warning of strange, unfamiliar noises. They bark when they hear other dogs barking. They can bark when they are frustrated, lonely, frightened, excited, or even when they are very happy.

Appropriate and moderate barking should be encouraged, and inappropriate and excessive barking discouraged. The basic obedience just learned must be used to teach your dog when it is appropriate to bark and when it isn't. If you want to discourage or eliminate barking completely, use the word NO and correct your dog with a leash, silencing any outcry swiftly and strongly.

Most owners, however, do not want to eliminate barking completely. They want to modify the behavior so the dog barks to warn them and then remains silent as he acknowledges the owner's validation of the person or situation the dog was warning about. A command that will quiet and relax the dog, showing that the owner is in control, may be enough. The command would be something like THAT'S ENOUGH; ENOUGH; RELAX; or GOOD BOY, QUIET. With some dogs, the owner will have to follow the command with some work in obedience routines, to lessen the dog's focus on what he was barking at and increase his focus on the obedience at hand. There are some dogs that are severe barkers in the home or, worse, in an apartment, where barking must be swiftly eliminated. In those cases, a severe leash correction on a choke chain, leaving no margin for misinterpretation, would be in order.

There are a number of special devices used for barking problems. Some are push-button, high-frequency ultrasound devices that only your dog can hear. These can distract your dog and can sometimes cause discomfort to its sensory nerves when activated. Some dogs on which these devices are used can end up neurologically compromised after a while. Other devices include Ultra Sonic Breakers that make a sharp noise that you can hear also. These often distract the dog's focus from the object he is barking at, but some dogs get used to the noise and soon bark again despite them.

Music or television programs serve to drown out some peripheral noises that dogs can bark at. Try to put on relaxing music on television shows. Don't, for example, put on nature shows about wolves or dogs in the wild. Your dog will start barking at the television instead of relaxing. Loud music is also not conducive to relaxation.

There are other devices known as electronic bark collars. They use varying intensities of electric shock to severely eliminate the barking problem. Do *not* use these devices! *In fact, never use any electric-shock devices on your own or any dog!*

Biting

Biting is a dog's one action that cannot be tolerated, because a dog is capable of inflicting tremendous damage with his bite. Most owners are not aware of this because the slight nips and scratches that are occasionally inflicted upon them by their own dogs lull them into thinking that that is all a dog is capable of. Actually, most dog owners never get to see, and are, therefore, not aware of, their dog's full biting potential. For example, the average two-year-old German shepherd weighing 65 pounds has a biting potential of from 400 to 700 pounds of pressure. Such a dog has the power in his jaws to easily break bones in your arms or legs or take a chunk a flesh out of any part of your body. Bigger dogs like St. Bernards have much more power behind their bites, and the ratings on them have exceeded 1,000 pounds of pressure. Of course, smaller dogs have a proportionately smaller biting potential. A small dog weighing between 25 and 35 pounds would exert less pressure—in such cases (only) 200 or 300 pounds. But even this size dog is capable of taking a finger cleanly off with one bite if he wants to.

Without trying to frighten you, the authors want everyone to realize fully the dangers that exist with biting dogs. Most biting problems are caused by dogs being hit, as an ineffective means of housebreaking, or put in some situation where they are teased. For instance, we know of a very sweet Great Dane puppy that was left alone in his fenced yard every day for a year at the approximate time that children were coming home from school. The children amused themselves daily by throwing sticks and rocks into the yard, all of which were aimed at the dog. The children also provided agitation by yelling at and teasing the dog as they went by. After a year of such treatment, this dog turned aggressive and tried to attack any child that got anywhere near it. What had happened was that this particular dog had been taught and conditioned to believe that the children existed only to torture and torment him. He was only responding to what he had learned. It took a great deal of time and expense to recondition the Great Dane, and the problem should never have been allowed to develop. It is an example of a good dog turned into a biter through no fault of his own.

Your dog's adult personality is shaped very early, when he is a puppy. Basically, when a dog is hit he will respond by biting. The greatest single cause of dogs' biting is *not* poor temperament, but mistreatment by misinformed owners that turns their lovable pets into defensive and aggressive potential threats to everyone.

Although biting is a severe problem, and cannot be tolerated, in most cases this negative behavior can be controlled or eliminated. Dogs will bite out of fear, aggression, confusion, pain, mental derangement, learned behavior (agitation), extreme excitement, as in predatory behavior, jealousy, competition over food or affection,

severe illness, and a myriad of other reason. They use their teeth to control or try to conquer what they perceive as a problem.

In general, the older the dog the more serious the biting problem can be. The longer the dog has been getting away with this, the harder it is to correct him. Also the larger the dog, the more serious the consequences of a bite. If members of the household are fearful, this can feed into the negative behavior. If members act erratically and scream, hit, run around, etc., this can worsen the problem.

Biting is most often a problem that should be dealt with by a professional trainer, who can, after questioning you and other family members comprehensively and getting a feel for the dog, give you specific recommendations for training your dog. A professional can help you understand why the dog is acting the way he is and how to retrain him.

Many dogs with biting problems are eventually given to the shelters to be put to sleep. This is a sad consequence of misbehavior which is usually caused by poor interaction with people, and can be cured or controlled with the correct action. Once again, it should be stressed that the biting problem is best approached as part of a sound obedience program. A good trainer will always be aware of this and work to change and modify the total behavior and perception of the dog towards the family members. If the people are out of control, or not respected, then chaos ensues. The household needs to earn, and keep, the respect of the dog, member by member, and day by day. A dog wants to know who is in control. If he is convinced he is, he will act accordingly. If he is convinced that you are, he will also act accordingly. Dogs can be very well controlled by and respect and obey only those who work them properly and earn their respect.

When dealing with dogs, keep in mind one important rule: *Never* hit your dog! If you have a puppy which has a tendency to bite, check the chapters pertaining to puppies, thereby correcting biting problems before they have a chance to escalate. If your dog has grown up and begun to bite, immediately follow the obedience routine in this book as it applies to the fearful biter and the aggressive dog.

Breeding the Female Dog

If you are considering breeding your dog, think long and hard and make sure you are doing it for the right reasons. It should be considered not only with a dog in good health and temperament, but one who will add favorably to the particular breed's gene pool. Don't decide to breed because you think you will make a lot of money. Most

Illus. 90. The stay hand signal and command follow the down command.

Illus. 91. The down correction when the trainer is six feet away.

Illus. 92. The optional alternative down-stay command and upraised hand signal from six feet away.

Illus. 93. The down-stay when the trainer is six feet away from the dog.

good breeders will often only break even for their efforts. Their primary intention is to improve the breed, not get rich.

Proper breeding requires a great deal of money. If you don't have enough money to give your dog (bitch) the proper nutrition—preferably at least 6 months before pregnancy—don't bother. You will have to sustain the bitch with proper nutrition not only through prebreeding, but through pregnancy, whelping, weaning, and her recovery period to normalcy. Skimping on nutrition anywhere along the way will increase the potential for trouble during motherhood, and can lead to great additional expense as a result of veterinarian bills, medication, and the possible losses of the pups or mother. You will also have to pay top dollar for a stud or arrange to give pick of the litter to quality breeders who have stud dogs to complement your dog's genetic background and temperament.

If you do not have enough time to devote to the entire process, then don't start. You have to be constantly available to see how the pups are doing; to hand-feed the pups in shifts if the litter is too big for mom; and to take care of one or more pups if they are considered runts and not fed properly or possibly even abandoned by the bitch.

Also, you have to have outlets (homes) for these puppies. This does not mean giving them away to the neighbors down the street or selling them to anyone who has the money for your high-priced breed. Are you prepared to interview and perhaps reject the prospective new owner of your pup; to have an ongoing and constructive dialogue with the new owners in which you will offer hints on diet, grooming, training, medical direction, and other assorted information which may be needed; and to take back the pup and refund the money if all does not go well?

You should also consider whether you have enough room for a new litter of pups as they grow, until they are finally placed in their new homes. The bigger the breed, the more room you need.

Also be aware that many breeders keep for a variety of reasons one or two dogs from each litter. This is a great expense and a great commitment.

One final note about breeding: The authors have had personal experience with specialized types of breeding such as all-natural-food rearing that uses no commercial foods, but a totally natural raw-food diet, and another specialized breeding in which only all-natural lacto-ovo vegetarian foods are given to the litter. Also, some breeders rear the litter naturally, using no vaccinations, but natural immune stimulators instead such as homeopathic and herbal preparations. These breeders want to carry on the genetic experiment for successive genera-

tions, to compare the results of their work with the more conventional approaches. Needless to say, this type of breeding brings with it the need for very specialized clientele and long-term record-keeping to keep track of the breeding procedures generated by the primary breeders.

Castrating the Male Dog

Many times, it is recommended by professionals that a male dog be castrated because of sexual behavior, the tendency to run away or urinate on the furniture, the dangerous habit of fighting with other dogs, the frustrating behavior of mounting people or other dogs, the manifesting of aggression, or the dog's propensity for testicular cancer. In some cases, castration could be considered a possible option; in others, it is not. Many times, owners will be hopeful of a quick fix, but this is the wrong approach to take. A better approach may be to examine the behavior itself to see if such a drastic solution is justified.

Some behavioral problems such as a dog fighting with other dogs and the possibilities of ripped body parts, including testicles, can justify castration. Some medical problems such as severe hormonal imbalance can lead to behavioral problems such as uncontrollable mounting, frequent penile erections, or spontaneous ejaculations. In such cases, castration may prove warranted.

The main rule to follow if you are considering castrating your dog is to avoid drastic irreversible solutions when simple ones will do. If your dog has a simple mounting problem, runs out of the house, or is moderately aggressive, approach it as a behavior problem which requires well-thought-out obedience solutions. If you don't understand the problem, you can't find the solution for it. But you always have the option of other more drastic measures later on.

As with any other obedience solution, the training framework has to be constructed first. Use the foundation of obedience training as described in this book to set the stage for the desired behavior modifications or changes. The dog must be convinced of your determination, effectiveness, and reliability. Some changes take more time than others.

One behavior pattern of a male dog that should be noted here occurs when he comes into proximity to a female dog in heat. He will go into a frenzy. And a male who has experienced a bitch or bitches in heat can become even more fevered in this environment. All males are tortured emotionally and physically by proximity to bitches in heat. They moan and howl. They can't rest, except when they are utterly exhausted. They can't concentrate on obedience training, or anything else, for that matter. They are singular of mind and purpose, and nothing less than gratification will do.

Even if a bitch is removed from them, male dogs take a long time to recover. The more frequently they are exposed to this torment, the longer they take to recover. We are convinced that you will take years off your dog's natural life span by subjecting him to this trauma. But the solution is not to castrate him. Often, even this drastic act does not eliminate the desire. A sire used often for breeding remembers the act even if he has been castrated. No, the solution to the problem lies in spaying the females in the household or removing the dog from this environment completely.

There are obvious reasons why female dogs in heat are not allowed in breed or obedience rings. A well-behaved dog and one trained at a high level can be controlled to override the distraction, but the emotional torture still exists.

If your dog is monorchid (one testicle descended) or cryptorchid (both testicles undescended), there may be many reasons to castrate him. If you breed a dog like this, his genes will pass more and more frequently into the gene pool. Don't breed a dog like this, no matter how lovely his temperament. If you have a normal sire who "throws" monorchid or cryptorchid males, you may want to castrate him in order to prevent other breeders from irresponsibly breeding these offspring. Some breeders withhold papers on unbreedable dogs until after they are spayed or castrated. Some won't place them until they are castrated. In some regions, even mixed breeds command good money. They can become the new "exotic" breed of tomorrow. Also, some breeders can always find ways of getting and falsifying papers, so until the last male is castrated, there is always a chance that he may someday be bred.

Dogs whose testicles reside deep within the body cavities, as opposed to being descended, are subject to testicular cancer. The constant increased heat of the body sets up a pathological process. If a dog has been allowed to develop the cancer, then surgery is even more of a pressing need. But the situation should be evaluated dog by dog, according to multiple factors that include age, condition, health, safety, etc.

We have personally trained very many intact dogs as well as quite a number of castrated males. We have not noticed a marked difference between the two concerning response and receptivity. It should be repeated one more time: Do not make a decision to castrate your dog as a quick fix to a problem. Examine all factors carefully.

Spaying the Female Dog

To spay or not to spay has always been a contentious argument among dog professionals and lay pet owners alike. Here we shall offer some insight from personal as well as extended professional experience.

Spaying is not for everyone. Some veterinarians are trying to make the decision easier for people by spaying pups at very early ages, before they are even placed in new homes.

If you do not plan to breed your dog, then you should seriously consider the option of spaying it. The procedure should be considered for a variety of reasons. One argument in favor of spaying is that overpopulation is producing unwanted dogs in almost catastrophic proportions, beckoning with it the massive compulsive killing of those same unwanted pets.

In making decisions to give your dog a hysterectomy, you should consider the age and health of the dog, the frequency of its heat cycles, the intensity and duration of its periods, the behavior of the dog in this time period, the other dogs in the household, both male and female, and the reputation and reliability of the veterinarian who will perform this procedure. Let's take these points one by one.

Let's assume you have acquired an 8- to 12-week-old puppy and you know you do not want to breed it. What is the ideal age to have this procedure done? With no complications, it can take anywhere from 10 to 20 minutes, on average, to perform a spay. We feel the dog is too young at 3 or 4 months of age to withstand any unnecessary or premature surgery.

Female dogs can come into heat generally from 6 months to a year old. This is the range for their first heat. They may come into heat or into season at 6 months and every 6 months after that, or they can go into a 9- or an 11-month cycle. Until after the first heat, we don't know when to ideally spay the dog, since she could be coming into heat anytime after 6 months. If you have your dog spayed arbitrarily, without knowing the timing, she could be coming into heat, and her uterus engorging with blood, thereby creating a much greater risk of hemorrhaging during surgery. This is the argument for waiting until around one month after the first heat to spay. The dog is young and strong and blood is not engorging the uterus. You would have to wait until the second heat to find out the frequency pattern.

The health of the dog should always be considered when thinking of elective surgery. It is always good to nutritionalize the pet even more potently than you normally would for about one month prior and one month after surgery. Basic nutrition boosting can include vitamin A or beta-carotene, vitamin B Complex, vitamin C Complex, vitamin E in capsules or liquid form, lecithin in granular or capsule form, and some garlic. These would be used according to the size of the dog.

Illus. 94. A front view of the down command at the six-foot distance.

Illus. 95. The recall.

If your dog's cycles occur more frequently—every 5 or 6 months as opposed to yearly—this may affect your decision to spay your dog. Each heat is a physical and emotional stress to the dog.

The intensity and duration of your dog's heat cycle are other considerations. If your female becomes very moody, depressed, amorous, or stops eating her food, this is not a good sign and eventually she will probably have more serious problems. If the heat drags on over three weeks or there is excessive staining, clotting, mucus discharge, or smell, it can mean trouble.

If her personality is somewhat too drastically changed during the heat, it can point to trouble. A Rottweiler or Great Pyrenees who is changing in personality can be frightening.

Other dogs in the household can suffer at the paws of a bitch in heat. She can become romantically involved with any female in the house, who may or may not be responsive to her advances. She may become aggressive to other bitches. She will torture any males in the household. They will be licking her urine, whining, pleading, crying, yowling, scratching and banging on doors. They will usually be "off their food" and maddeningly single-minded in their quest for gratification. This situation, repeated even several times, can seriously shorten the life of any male dog and lead to serious health problems. The house is usually not big enough to contain healthfully the male dog and the bitch in heat. Please don't ever try to.

Spaying is the most common surgery done by veterinarians. A veterinarian who cannot do a good spay shouldn't be let near any knives. Check around and ask for some references of happy and satisfied clients. This should not be an insult to the veterinarian; if this request should create hostility, seek help elsewhere.

One of the most horrendous and expensive results, in terms of cost and health, of not spaying your dog is the pyometra. This is a massive pus flow that builds in the uterus, requiring major surgery. It often develops in silence and can present itself with alarming severity in a heartbeat of time. A pyometra can be open (draining) or closed (not draining). Either is serious, but a closed pyometra can often result in death from massive infection. Mammary tumors are also more prevalent in unspayed females. These often turn cancerous.

There is always an anesthetic risk with any surgery. But all things considered, if you assess all the advantages and disadvantages of spaying your dog, you may consider spaying to be the lesser of the two evils. Whatever your decision, make it after learning as much about this subject as possible.

Cat Chasing

If your dog's hunting instinct is sparked when a car goes by, then it is surely kindled when a cat runs by. Some dogs are almost powerless to resist chasing an animal that is running away from them. Since it is a natural instinct for almost any dog, it will take persistence and consistency on your part to discourage your dog from indulging in this irresistible compulsion.

Work your dog in the complete obedience routine outlined in the obedience-training section of this book, utilizing cats as frequent distractions, until finally your dog can work very close to them. This will change his attitude towards cats from something that should be chased to just another distraction to be ignored.

You can worsen your dog's tendency for cat-chasing by staking or tying your dog outside on a line, while a cat or cats walk by cautiously, or sometimes in a taunting manner. Cats are unaware that such behavior may be dangerous to them. They can't judge the distance and speed with which a dog can pounce on them and go for the lethal kill. This is a horrific thing to watch, and it changes your attitude towards your dog.

Some dogs such as terriers and sighthounds have a very high predatory drive and pursue cats for the joy of the chase. (Sighthounds are breeds of dogs who are able to see their prey from far away.) In other cases, the dog as a puppy may have been scratched or dominated by a cat, and as an adult has decided not to take the torture anymore.

If you leave your dog tied up with loose cats outside, it is only a matter of time before tragedy strikes. But be assured it will happen. The dog has plenty of time to study the cat's behavior. He knows the prize will be his, with patience. If this scenario is happening to you, it is cruel indeed to let it continue. Once your dog has caught a cat, he can extend his chases to rabbits, squirrels, birds, ferrets, and even smaller dogs. More and more little creatures can become prey.

Work your obedience training thoroughly in specific situations, but don't expect your dog to reliably carry over what he has learned from training session to training session if you leave him alone for hours.

Cat chasing in the home can also be a devastating problem. For starters, don't let your cat or cats tease or scratch a young dog introduced into a new household with cats established in it already. So often, owners feel, foolishly, that cats and dogs will work out their problems on their own, without interference. Do you really think that the four walls of a house will automatically, and by themselves, civilize two animals involved in a primal, predatory relationship? The law of the jungle will prevail, unless you prevent the confrontation before it begins.

So don't allow hatred to develop. If your cat is stalking your dog, spray the cat in the face with a water gun. Don't give your dog this correction. Stop any predatory behavior on the part of the dog by using your basic obedience routine to build the proper relationship with the dog, and then use the silent about-turn corrections on the long line to make his pursuit of the cat a very unpleasant activity.

Some dogs will never be trustworthy around cats. They will let cats rub up against them, but when the cat starts to run, they will pounce upon them. They will also wait to attack the cat when it sniffs the dog's food and/or water bowl, or climbs into the dog's crate, or attempts to jump on the kitchen counters to get water or food. Some cats can sit harmoniously for hours with a dog by a windowsill, but when they go to the litter box to start urinating and defecating can meet an untimely end. Dogs don't like to eat their own stool, but almost always love to eat cat stool as the cat is defecating. In such situations, the cat will turn around and attack, to its own disadvantage. Many a cat gets sick, and the owner never knows why, because in a dog-and-cat household the cat can never go to the bathroom in peace. It begins to hold it in, or go in places that the dog can't get to. It would be much better for the cat if the owner realized that the cat needs an area in which to eat, urinate, and defecate alone. Provide places on counters for food and litter boxes, or leave a room or basement door open just enough for a cat to go back and forth, without the dog being able to pursue it.

Booda boxes can be death traps for cats. As they are leaving, the dog may be entering, and a fight will ensue. If you are at all in doubt as to your dog's trustworthiness in any or all of these situations, do not allow your dog and cat to interact unsupervised. They won't get along; your dog will know when things are favorable for an attack and he will take full advantage.

There are many many factors at play in cat-chasing and cat-and-dog interactive behavior. If in doubt, enlist the help of a good professional trainer who is well versed in these things.

Chewing

Adult dogs can have lasting chewing problems. We expect most puppies to have chewing problems because they are babies, in the midst of discovery. Part of the way they discover, as with human babies, is through taste, feel, and smell. Puppies are also teething and try to relieve pressure on their swollen gums by gnawing on all types of objects. But this behavior should, for the most part, have worked itself out by the time the dog is a year old.

It should be pointed out that dogs don't automatically outgrow the need for chew toys, so it's safe to assume that more adult dogs than not will enjoy indulging in oral aerobics at least now and then. That being the case, safe, effective, and appropriate chewing toys should be provided for their gratification. Among the natural bones are sterilized beef bones that come in all different sizes and thicknesses. These can be used by your dog and then washed over and over for long-term use. Avoid using butcher bones. Their marrow could be questionable for the dog's health. The bones could split or splinter, causing grave problems to the dog's digestive system. Remember, bones from fresh-killed prey are much softer and easier to digest than cooked and dehydrated bones from the meat market.

Whichever natural bones you use, try to get the thickest you can, all around. Don't buy bones with many spongy holes or hairline cracks. Buy bones larger than you'd think appropriate for your dog's mouth. A bone larger than your dog's mouth has a better chance of not breaking, fracturing, or splintering into dangerous slivers that your dog will automatically eat.

Nylon-type bones which are ham- or beef-scented are also very good chew toys, providing hours of safe chewing enjoyment. They can also be washed and sterilized, minimizing the threat of teeth and gum infection.

There are hard-rubber Cressite toys that can be appropriate for some of the smaller breeds. New, improved chew toys are always coming out on the market. Check with your regional pet suppliers for type and variety. In general, try to avoid toys that splinter, crack, break, crumble, fall apart, have dangerous parts which pets can swallow and choke on, can't be cleaned, or are cheap enough to throw away. If your dog wants to chew but doesn't like your selection, then you can try rubbing olive or tuna oil, cheese, or chicken or bacon fat on the toys as an extra incentive for him to work out the chewing behavior.

If your dog is chewing along edges of couches, mattresses, and cushions, or the adult chewing problem is recent and not typical of your dog's behavior, look to some medical conditions with your dog's teeth. Check for bleeding or receding gums, foul-breath odor, excess tartar, abscesses, cracked teeth, loose teeth, or for food or other objects caught between teeth. If there is a medical problem, this must be taken care of before you can hope to cure the chewing problem.

It has become very popular to brush your dog's teeth nowadays. This is a very beneficial thing to do. Buy a soft-bristle toothbrush for your dog. Be sure to keep it

Illus. 96. The trainer is giving the recall command and hand signal while bending forward slightly.

Illus. 97. This dog is sitting too far out in front.

separate from those for other members of the household. Also keep a separate toothbrush for each dog. Color-code them if you like. You can use a variety of things on the toothbrush. Aloe gel, which can be bought in health-food stores, works great by itself or with some vitamin C powder. A 3% solution of hydrogen peroxide, found in drugstores, also works well by itself or with some baking soda. Most pet suppliers now have a kit for cleaning your pet's teeth. You can try that also. Depending upon how bad the teeth, how quickly they form tartar, and how sensitive the gums are, you can clean your dog's teeth anywhere from once a day to once a week.

Chewing in adult dogs can be caused by anxiety, boredom, frustration, or anger. Adult dogs become anxious because they do not like being left alone. They suffer separation anxiety. They have been used to company all day long, only to suffer the loss of that companionship when both husband and wife have to go to work or the children go off to summer camp or college. New adjustments must be made and anxiety sets in.

If your dog has developed anxiety because he has been left alone, a good thing to do is give him the well-flavored chew toys right before you leave the house. Most of the anxiety chewing is done within the first 15 minutes of the owner leaving the house. If you can offer a highly enticing distraction to get the dog over the initial leaving, then you have a better chance of resolving this problem. Ambience is important also. Try to leave soft, continuous music on, or an appropriate TV program. No nature programs to drive the dog crazy, however!

It helps to build up the time slowly that the dog is left alone, and vary that time. Vary these periods so they are sometimes of short duration and sometimes of long, so the dog won't anticipate having to cope with always being alone for long periods.

Make your returns pleasant, and give some quality attention to the dog when you return. They live for this. Perhaps some petting, a long walk, or a gentle massage will fulfill your dog's needs. If he is very excited, don't feed him right away. Let your dog calm down first. If you come back home, look around and find destruction, and then yell and scream after the destruction has been done, you will build up even more anxiety in your dog. If the dog is not reliable or becomes unreliable after being left loose in the entire household, then confine him to a more appropriate area. Try to determine what might be the most likely objects for destruction beforehand, and spray some bitter-tasting preparations on them before you leave. Pet stores have a variety of chewing repellents to choose from. These preparations need to be renewed daily. Make things you don't want chewed taste bad, and things you do want chewed taste good.

Dogs that are terribly destructive could be a danger to themselves as well as devastating to the household. In severe cases, you may want to confine your dog to a crate. If your dogs chew on wires or other dangerous items, they must be confined when you are away. Even with initial crate confinement, you can work your dog into more freedom gradually.

Self-Mutilation

Dogs who chew ruthlessly on their own bodies are sadly becoming all too common these days. Dogs mutilate themselves for many reasons. They may be nervous, bored, hurting, or itching, or a collar may be ill-fitted and annoying them. They may be having an allergic reaction to parasites, pollen, pollutants, medications, supplements, food, water, perfumes, soaps, shampoos, baths, dips, clothing, etc. It is very important to not simply go the antibiotic and cortisone route without first trying to find out what has gone wrong. You have to determine if the pancreas, adrenal glands, bowels, kidneys, and lungs are functioning properly.

The skin is the largest eliminative organ of the body. When the body is overloaded with toxins of any kind, from any source, the skin will help out with the ordinary as well as extraordinary elimination. This can be troublesome and discomforting to your dog. Once he feels the discomfort, even slightly, and starts to react by chewing in an attempt to relieve it, the secondary problems—bruising, infection, pulling and losing his hair—become much more serious than the initial problem. These complications can happen all too quickly, as many pet owners have experienced. Since this discomfort and the subsequent mutilation can happen so quickly, it's a very good idea to inspect the skin on your dog, if not daily, then at least weekly. You can accomplish this while grooming, massaging, or petting him. It will be both enjoyable and informative. If something causes your dog to start chewing himself, waste no time in finding the cause and correcting it.

There are many ways to cure your dog's itching and stop his chewing. Start with external remedies. Using a good massage and increasing the blood supply to the skin surface and thereby eliminating toxins is a very good start. Ensuring that your dog's skin is clean is also important. Use a natural, mild shampoo, letting it be absorbed into the skin surface for 5 to 10 minutes. While massaging the shampoo into your dog's skin is very important, thorough rinsing is essential, as soap residue can cause irritation and chewing all over again. A final rinse with peroxide and water or cider vinegar and water in the ratio of 1 part peroxide or cider vinegar to about 7 parts water is common and effective. Keep this solution away from your dog's eyes. Putting aloe gel on a hot, wet washcloth and rubbing it all over your dog's body is also very effective.

Using a tea solution of herbs such as chamomile, echinacea, goldenseal, red clover, red raspberry, and/or rosemary is also effective. Dilute two teabags in two quarts of hot water. Let it cool and pour it over the dog. For isolated areas of trouble you can rub on lemon, witch hazel, peroxide, aloe gel, raw potato, onion or cucumber, bentonite clay, raw honey, olive oil, or vitamin E. There are many natural ways to handle chewing problems.

One way to approach this internally is to use homeopathic preparations such as graphite, sulfur, hepar sulph, ferrum Phos, silica, Hydrastis and many other ingredients. Consult a veterinary homeopathic *Materia Medica* for specifics. Another approach is to use basic vitamin and mineral supplements which can be obtained at any health food store. These include vitamin A, an animal source such as halibut liver oil or cod liver oil, beta-carotene (the vegetable source of vitamin A), some B Complex or Spirulina or green magma, blue-green algae wheatgrass or barley grass, or a combination of bee pollen, vitamin C and bioflavonoids with vitamin E, and lecithin. You can consult a multitude of veterinary nutrition books for specifics on quantities and potencies. There are also many herbal preparations which can be used internally such as corn silk, couch grass, red clover, yucca, goldenseal, arrowroot, red raspberry, and peppermint. Consult a good herbal health guide for very specific advice as to quantities and frequency.

The holistic approach is being more and more accepted and applied to veterinary medicine the world over. There are many options using these approaches that don't harm and can greatly benefit the immune system and basic constitution of the dog.

Dog's Behavior in Car

Cars are fun places for some dogs, and absolutely horrible places for other dogs. Whether your dog is deliriously happy or extremely fearful in a car, it is essential from a safety standpoint that he behave properly. Cars are dangerous places to be if the dog pounces and jumps about mindlessly or gets excited when he sees another dog or other animals. To ensure the proper behavior from your dog in the car you must convince him that you can control him, even at times when, in fact, you can't.

Your dog should have been worked in the basic obe-dience procedures before you try to control him in the car. You must have demonstrated to him that you are effective and consistent in your commands before he will even think of listening to you in the precarious and animated environment of the car. If you approach the car with an out-of-control dog, don't expect to gain any semblance of control in the car.

Here are some things you should avoid doing when planning to take your dog on a car trip: Don't feed your dog two to three hours before a car ride. Don't pile your dog in with the whole family before working some one-on-ones with him. Don't let your dog drink excessively before riding. Don't make beginning rides very long ones. Don't let your dog ride in a very cold car. Don't let your dog bounce around from front to back seat. Don't let your dog ride in the front seat, passenger side. Don't let your dog ride on your lap. Don't let your dog lick your face while you drive. Don't let your dog paw your arm while you drive. Don't let your dog slap you senseless, in the back of the head with his paw or his muzzle, while you drive. Don't let your dog tap-dance among the brake and accelerator pedals. Don't let your dog eat in the car or gnaw on the car upholstery. Don't allow your dog to hang his head out the window while you are driving. It is dangerous and subjects him to eye irritations and infections. Don't expect to control your dog in the car unless he has a leash and collar on.

Don't let your dog breathe excess carbon monoxide fumes in a closed car. Leave windows slightly open in all weather. Don't just take your dog for rides to the veterinarian or boarding kennel, take him to fun places. Take him to a variety of places, and vary the length of the trips.

Don't leave things in the car for your dog to get tangled in and destroy. Don't leave your dog in the car alone with a leash and collar that he can get tangled up in and choke on. Don't leave your dog alone in the car in an area where you can't watch him. Don't leave your dog in an area where he may be stolen or agitated.

Don't reprimand your dog if he gets sick in the car and vomits or has diarrhea. *Do* think about using herbal or homeopathic preparations on your dog in the car to combat anxiety, nervousness, or car sickness.

Obedience Training for the Car

Put the proper leash and collar on your dog and make him heel by the car. Make him sit and stay with the door closed. Then slowly open the door, still requiring him to sit and stay. Close the door and do an about-turn, having him heel away with you. As you do another about-turn,

Illus. 98. The dog is sitting in front of the trainer correctly after the re-call command.

Illus. 99. The dog heeling off the leash.

work your way to the car. If he lunges forward, to get to the car, do your quick right about-turns again and again till you are moving once more towards the car. When your dog sits and stays, open the door and then release your dog into the backseat with the word OKAY. Get into the front seat and, holding the leash, command your dog to sit and stay. Praise him with the words GOOD BOY. If your dog gets too excited, use verbal praise only.

Heel your dog outside the car and repeat the procedure all over again. When you open the door, release him with the word OKAY into the backseat and command him, SIT, STAY. Now, drop your dog into the down position with an upraised hand since you have gained some control with the sit-stay and you have his attention. Continue these exercises, alternating the sit-stays with downs. Move on until your dog releases on the word OKAY and obeys the DOWN command.

Work your dog until you feel you have good control over him in the driveway or by the curb. The you must enlist an aide who will get in the driver's seat and move the car up and down the driveway or around the block slowly. You should be in the passenger seat and have your dog in the backseat. First, even make sure you have control over the dog with just the engine running and the car not moving.

Next, establish control over your dog while the car is moving. Proceed this way for a while, until your dog shows you he can behave in a moving vehicle for short rides at moderate speed. Continue to elevate the difficulty for him by having longer and more enticing rides and distractions. You should be in the passenger seat, ready to correct your dog for any infractions.

Eventually, you will come to the point where you will change positions with your helper, and you will drive the car and he will correct your dog. The dog must see that control is effective no matter who is doing the driving, and who is doing the correcting. Then the big moment will arrive where you will try driving with your dog in the backseat on your own. Drive up and down the driveway, or make rights turns on a local street. If your dog makes any infractions, yell NO, DOWN! If your dog does not follow these commands promptly, calmly but quickly stop the car and turn towards your dog, giving him a leash correction and the NO command, as simultaneous correction, in a downward direction. If your dog does not lie down, give him a new command, and if he does not obey this command give him the DOWN correction and start alternating the corrections with the commands.

When you have control, let your dog see that you can drive off again, fully in control even though only you are in the car. Persistence and consistency will reap rewards in all situations. At toll booths, drop your dog into a down-stay; do not seize him, mid-leap, lunging for the toll taker. Happy travelling!

Fighting

Fighting between dogs is very dangerous and a tough problem to stop. Certain breeds are more prone to fighting than others. This behavior is usually cultivated in some dogs at an early age, when they are attacked by other dogs. Once the fighting instinct is kindled, it becomes a permanent part of the dog's personality and is very difficult to eradicate.

A dog that is a confirmed fighter represents an extreme danger to his owner, other people, and other dogs. The habit must be stopped early and not be given a chance to grow. Fighting dogs should never be given the opportunity to make physical contact with other dogs. Work them with the obedience routine, concentrating on using other dogs as distractions, until they can be worked near other dogs and their attitude towards others improves. Since this behavior is an extremely dangerous problem, give your dog very severe corrections.

One way to prevent your dog from fighting is to prevent him from making contact, friendly or otherwise, with other dogs. Dogs will fight with dogs of both sexes. Also, the size of the dog makes no difference. Small dogs will fight large dogs. Large dogs will fight with even larger dogs. Fighting can start as playing, progress to play-fighting, and then escalate to real fighting.

Dogs don't have to have many fights to become seasoned fighters. One bad fight can contaminate your dog for life. Dogs aren't only dangerous with the dog they had the fight with. They can pick on strange dogs or even turn on dogs they are friendly with. Dogs don't care what human is around, begging and pleading with them to stop. They will not listen to you, when in the thick of the fray. You must physically separate the dogs by pulling them away from each other with leash control if you have it, or pulling them off each other by lifting the back legs of both dogs. It takes two people to do this. If one person tries to break up a fight, this usually leads to trouble. Dogs in the middle of a fight don't care what they bite, including you. So you can be in great danger, and you can be injured, but you will have to move quickly and decisively, in order to avoid a total disaster. The dogs are still in a frenzied state when separated, and can take out their frustrations on the nearest thing: you, some other person, or some other animal. Try to throw the dogs into separate crates or rooms, so they will calm down. Serious fighting or fighting that occurs more than once dictates the help of a competent professional in the area.

With or without a professional, the key to changing your dog's behavior begins with gaining his respect. This comes about through the relationship you build in basic obedience as described in this book. When this relationship is formed, you will have the beginning tools for conquering almost any problem that comes up.

Reasons for Fighting

Dogs will fight for many reasons, including for the affection of someone, over food or a female dog, for defensive purposes, to protect a person or area, and to establish dominance. The best way to avoid serious fights is to be aware of all the reasons why these fights occur and try to prevent any of these situations from occurring.

Let's start with territory. A dog is territorial. He will fight to protect where he lives; this area can extend to the yard. Your dog is more likely to fight to defend his place than to defend neutral or unfamiliar ground.

Dogs also get jealous as people do, with some of the same unruly consequences. Two dogs can always be potentially jealous of the attentions of one or more masters. Each dog may have a favorite person, or both dogs may have the same favorite person. Size up the situation and do not reward jealous behavior with cutesy statements such as "Ah, he's jealous, isn't that adorable?" See the potential danger for what it is and act accordingly.

Jealous behavior should be rewarded with a leash correction and a sharp NO, followed by a sojourn into the obedience routine. If the dog acts acceptably when released and understands that jealousy has no place in your household, reward him with affection. Should the dog behave in an aggressive manner towards the other dog, another correction and more obedience work are in order. Continue until you feel your dog is showing the spirit of cooperation.

If there are two people involved and two dogs showing aggression towards each other, both people must assert control and displeasure over this display, correcting both dogs with the word NO and following with obedience routines for both. The two people involved should work each of the dogs apart from, and then close to, one another. Each must gain respect from each dog, and shouldn't play favorites.

If the jealous behavior involves children, the adult or adults must take control, unless the child or children are old enough to handle the work at hand. If only one dog is the aggressor, then work only that one dog as a correction for this behavior. But work both or all dogs in a household in obedience work. If you were to work only one dog in a household, say typically, a new puppy, and the older dog were left to his own devices, it could result

in even more domination by the established dog because you are dominating the puppy but no one is dominating the older dog. Equalize the relationship by training all the dogs. Have all mature members of the household work them all. They may behave with deference to the human head of the household who had earned their respect, but very differently with a teenager who may be disinterested in the order of things.

There was a recent news item concerning a woman who knifed a man in a restaurant for picking at food in her plate. Clearly this couple had a problem with sharing food, and so do dogs. All dogs deserve a clean, private, place in which to eat. They should not have to share a bowl, eat so fast as to not let another dog get to it, or give up on eating altogether because a dominant dog will wander over and lick the plate clean. Each dog should eat at his own pace, and feel secure with his food.

Fights also occur over females even when not in heat. For example, a son may fight his father to gain sexual standing with his mother; or a female may have a favorite male partner, but the other male in the household, undaunted, remains persistent. The potential for fighting increases even more with dogs in heat.

Defense of a person or persons a dog loves can be a rational or irrational catalyst for a dog fight. Dogs who are secure in their relationship with you and understand that they must obey your commands will be much less likely to overreact in defending you from some perceived danger. Dogs who are nervous and insecure can make mistakes. When in doubt, they will fight.

Every time a new dog enters the household, the social hierarchy changes. You cannot assume that the established dog will be more dominant. He may try at first, and be worn down by the temperament, size, persistence, or strength of the newcomer or by age and health factors. Don't assume your dog needs company, and that any new dog will be good for him. He may want to be alone. If he doesn't, be careful about which companion you choose. Some new companions may be good for him, and some may be bad. Some may start out bad and turn out good.

Remember that adding or subtracting dogs from a household will affect everyone involved. Some dogs can get healthier with the new addition. Some dogs can get sicker. Some dogs feel they are constantly called upon to defend their position and so become very nasty and irritable. Others yield to the situation and waste away in despair. Many owners are amazed at the personality changes in their dogs when additions and subtractions occur. It is common for an owner to remark that he does not seem to recognize his dog.

Strong prey drive is a primal, compelling behavior in

Illus. 100. The dog obeying the sit-stay command off the leash at the full six-foot distance.

Illus. 101. The dog obeying the down-stay command off the leash at the heel position.

dogs. Some display this drive very strongly, some moderately (if the prey happens to be very convenient), and some seemingly not at all. Observe your dog's body posture when out for a walk. How does he react to squirrels, rabbits, cats, or other small animals? If he lunges towards potential prey, crouches low, stares intently, springs forward, screams, whines, barks, growls, or acts agitated in other ways, you must be extremely careful.

Terrible fights can occur between two dogs you are walking at the same time if they see something they want to pursue. Not being able to get at the object of their drive, they can very well turn on each other in frustration. This can also occur if only one dog displays predatory behavior. When frustrated, he can still take it out on the dog walking with him.

As you can see, we could write an entire book about dog fighting, but we won't here. Suffice it to say, be very mindful of all the warnings we have given you, and use your own common sense and intuition to prevent problems before they occur.

Fleas

Flea infestation of household pets, and their owners, is rapidly reaching epidemic proportions. We humans, blessed with wisdom and compassion in many areas, sit ruefully by, watching our beloved pets being served up as the main course to a flourishing army of voracious little parasites. The flea problem is shrouded in misinformation. We can no longer afford to ignore it while our sentient furry friends suffer the backlash of our ignorance.

Fleas are parasites, and as parasites their role in the scheme of things is to scavenge the blood of sick organisms. By singling out the sick, parasites help to return these organisms to the earth from whence they came, in order for nature to ensure the continuation of healthy organisms. Parasites play a very important role in nature. Without them, we would be smothered in a proliferation of unchecked animal and vegetable filth.

When animals are in a state of vitality, nature does not have to compensate with these tireless parasites. But when man has violated the health of those creatures in his keeping, by feeding them diets replete with chemicals, coloring, hormones, pesticides, what other consequence could there be but widespread disease or illness? Disease is the body ill at ease. It is a condition created by the body as a remedial effort. Maintain the factors conducive to illness, and illness will always prevail. Maintain the factors conducive to health, and vitality will prevail. Animals who are infested with fleas, internal parasites, allergies, or other skin problems are sick ani-

mals. Fleas obtain blood from their prey by sawing into its flesh with their mouths. They then inject from their saliva a decoagulant into the animal to thin its blood, making it easier to draw the blood up into their bodies. It is this fluid—which contains viruses, pathogenic bacteria, and blood parasites from every other sick animal the fleas have feasted upon—that causes moderate to severe reactions, sometimes referred to as saliva allergies. These saliva allergies are diagnosed as summer eczema, fungal infestation, mange, or any number of nonspecific allergies.

There is a wide variance in individual skin sensitivity to the flea bite. One animal may react severely for days and weeks after being bitten a few times, while another animal who has been feasted upon may seem unaware of it. Also, allergic reactions may appear right away or days after the bite. It depends partly on the vitality of the animal and the way the poison is eliminated from its body. The skin is a very frequently used vehicle, since it is the largest eliminative organ. However, a dog with no skin problems is not necessarily a dog in good health. This could also mean that the dog is too weak to throw off the poisons in this way, and perhaps has even greater difficulty eliminating toxins through other channels. If you can't find fleas on your animal, but he is scratching, biting, and perhaps causing licking sores, fleas could be the problem. But you are not likely to find a tiny infestation.

When an animal is devitalized and becomes ill, he becomes ideal prey for the flea. A diseased body sends signals that attract fleas. As fleas invade the host tissue, the host becomes weaker. Flea bites cause irritation, which causes the host to scratch. As your dog or cat does this, he breaks down his skin. Now the fleas increase their feeding frenzy. As more adult females feed, they lay more eggs. These eggs bounce off the animal into the surrounding bedding and floor crevices, hatching in a few days. This hatching is known as the maggot or larval stage. Larvae feed upon adult flea excreta, known as blood crumbs, which is being produced continually as the adult fleas feed.

Larvae reach maturity in about ten days, in which time they spin a cocoon around themselves for protection and enter into the pupa stage. Fleas in the egg and pupa stages are fairly resistant to chemicals, whereas the larval and adult stages are the most vulnerable.

Fleas can pupate over the winter in your home and emerge as full-fledged ravenous adults with the first blush of spring. Fleas cannot see or walk, but they feel vibrations of approaching living organisms and proceed to jump around wildly, until they reach their objective, a warm-blooded host. Fleas and other blood-sucking insects are intermediate parasites and as such are disinterested in dead matter. Dogs intuitively comprehend the role of parasites, and to prevent fleas from attacking them will roll about in putrid, decaying filth. In this way, they are attempting to render themselves unacceptable to the fleas.

Treatments

There are nutritional approaches we can undertake instead of rolling our dogs in filth. Two old standbys are brewer's yeast and raw-grated fresh garlic. The garlic exudes sulfur through the skin, which acts as a natural repellent to fleas. Brewer's yeast and garlic also contain zinc, which heals eczema and other skin problems. Brewer's yeast can be used topically also.

Eliminate commercial foods totally if possible. Favorable foods include yogurt, cottage cheese, eggs, ricotta, tofu, mozzarella, feta, Gouda, Edam, and Muenster cheese, kefir, buttermilk, raw cow's or goat's milk, and other wholesome dairy products. Vegetables of the mustard-oil family, including garlic, onions, scallions, radishes, watercress, mustard greens, carrots, beets, cucumbers, parsley, peppers, eggplant, dandelion, celery, etc., should be daily additions to the main protein.

There is one axiom that is worth remembering at this point: Disease causes germs, germs do not cause disease. Germs or bacteria can mutate from friendly inhabitants into pathogens, and back to friendly ones again. Essentially, the bacteria react to the medium in which they live. Bacteria are capable of mutation. If your animal has a proliferation of pathogenic micro-organisms in his body, it is because conditions have led to the accumulation of viruses (filth).

Germs have never been isolated outside of the body. They are not out there riding piggyback on a particle of dust, waiting to seize your pet with some as yet unknown devastating infection. Germs have been isolated only in *diseased living tissue*. The myriad microbe hunters of our prestigious research institutions have truly found germ bacteria in diseased tissue. They have almost unilaterally concluded that if germs are present in diseased tissue, then germs must indeed be the culprit of disease. Unfortunately, this is convoluted logic.

Along with dairy products and fresh vegetables, also give your dog every day fresh sprouts from a seed-sprouting mix which you cultivate yourself. About one cup daily is a good guide for a fifty-pound dog. Some of the sprouts which you can obtain easily in about three days are from wheat berries, rye berries, alfalfa, lentils, mung beans, buckwheat, radishes, red clover, and fennel. A variety of these can be mixed together and sprouted simultaneously. One fruit meal a day in the morning is also helpful.

For optimum health, cut out all red meat and supplement the dairy proteins, if desired, with organic chicken or turkey—if possible fresh-cooked and not out of a can. Tofu (soy bean curd) is a very easy protein to digest, although it is rather bland to the taste at first and may need the addition of some grated cheese or natural tomato sauce.

Include the following additions to your pet's breakfast during the week only if your animal is not sick or very infested with fleas: whole, unrefined, organically grown grains, soaked for five to ten minutes in fresh vegetable juice; raw milk or rejuvilac (fermented wheat berries); and a granola mix which can include cornmeal, thinly rolled oats, wheat flakes, rye flakes, soy flakes, triticale flakes, barley flakes, raw-grated sunflower seeds, wheat germ, raw, ground-up peanuts, carob powder or kibble, coconut, lecithin, and nutritional yeast. Make small quantities of this granola and refrigerate it, since some ingredients are perishable. If your dog's digestion is poor or the animal is weak or getting on in age, add digestive enzymes and friendly flora (complex bacteria) via *lactobacillus bifidus*.

One day out of every week impose a fast. This can be a modified fast consisting completely of fresh cut-up fruits, vegetable juices, or distilled water with some raw honey, or of giving your dog just a breakfast meal with nothing until breakfast the next day. From breakfast of one day to breakfast of the next day, allow your dog's body to cleanse itself while it remains free of the task of processing food.

The body consumes the least useful materials first. A fasting body is not a starving body. The objective is to make the body cleanse and rebuild itself, creating greater resistance to all manner of disease. We want the animal so healthy that the fleas will flee in disinterest.

For flea prevention as well as control, herbs should also be a daily part of the cleansing and nourishing regime. Include such popular ones as alfalfa, kelp comfrey, rosemary, thyme, sage garlic, and a bit of cayenne pepper. Many others are also important for specific purposes, but it would take a book to elaborate upon these herbs. Unsaturated fatty acids can be given daily, via good expeller oils such as sunflower, olive, sesame, safflower, and peanut oil. Controlling fleas through nutrition will require varying amounts of time, depending first upon the state of the animal's health and also how stringently you are committed to following the new dietary regime. Do not expect overnight success!

Flea collars can also be used to control fleas. The active agent in most flea collars is either dichlorvos or

Illus. 102. The dog obeying the down-stay command off the leash at the full six-foot distance.

Illus. 103. The dog obeying the recall command off the leash.

dioxin (a byproduct of Agent Orange). These chemicals work on the principle of dermal absorption, which leads ultimately to blood poisoning or blood toxemia. The chemicals in the collar are absorbed primarily through the skin of the animal, although dogs can also breathe in and swallow their insidious effects. The idea in using the collar is that when the flea attempts to feast on the dog, the blood of the animal will be sufficiently polluted to cause the death of the flea. Admittedly, this is a very drastic technique. What's worse, resistant strains of fleas are created, since some will get only small amounts of poison and reproduce stronger, more resistant strains. The pesticides will not generally kill fleas during their first three stages, anyway.

Less drastic techniques can be used, although they are more time-consuming. Fleas will die in very hot water. Some will also be asphyxiated in soapsuds, although many others will hide in the matted hairs of the animal. This is why it is also important to make sure your dog's hair is not matted and your dog is as well-groomed as possible. You can use a good olive oil or herbal bar soap that suds up well, or a liquid herbal shampoo. Create a good lather, and leave it on your dog for five to ten minutes. While the suds are plentiful, run a flea comb through the animal and quickly drown all caught fleas in a nearby pan of hot water or alcohol. Finish off with a mild cider/vinegar rinse of seven parts water to one part vinegar, or fresh lemon juice and distilled water using the same proportions of water to lemon. Make a quart to a gallon of this rinse, depending upon the size of the dog, and leave it on as the final rinse. Do not use this juice rinse on animals with open lesions and raw skin. It will burn too much.

Another remedy that can be used is to pick a handful of one or two herbs such as rosemary, sage, thyme, or eucalyptus leaves, and place it in boiling water. Lower the temperature of the water until it reaches room temperature. Drain the water and pour the herbs over the animal as a final rinse. Several times daily keep combing the animal and catching the fleas in a nearby pot of *very hot* water or alcohol. Repellant oils can also be used in the water.

You also need to attack fleas during their egg, larvae, and pupa stages. The simplest and safest method of accomplishing this is to pour boiling water lavishly all over kennel runs and wherever dogs and cats are likely to sleep. This will kill fleas at all four stages. Rugs and areas not conducive to the boiling-water treatment will require thorough vacuuming. Throw out used vacuum bags, because the fleas can develop inside them. Old bedding and blankets should be washed or discarded. Some small pillows may be washed, vacuumed, or heated in a two-hundred-degree oven for about fifteen minutes.

Animals with heavy flea infestation must be thoroughly combed several times daily with a flea comb, which will catch the adults for disposal in a nearby dish of hot water, alcohol, or repellant oils in water (ten to fifteen drops of orange, rosemary, eucalyptus, citronella, or pennyroyal will serve nicely).

Herbal flea collars can be worn at all times as a preventive measure. If the dog is in a heavily infested area, such as the warm, moist climate of much of Florida and California, you can mix an herbal powder brew which will be useful as an additional deterrent to fleas. The mix can contain equal parts of rosemary, thyme, garlic, and a little red pepper thrown in for good measure. Mix all these herbs in powder form in a bowl. Put them into a salt shaker with large holes and sprinkle the mixture on the dog daily, especially before taking him out. Fleas don't appreciate getting these herbs stuck in their mouths, and so will leave the scene for more palatable fare. Should the dog lick off some of this herbal mixture, it will help to provide some additional internal protection. Another approach is to brew this mixture as you would tea and, when it is lukewarm, drain it and then pour it over your dog, letting it air-dry.

There are other aids you can use for flea control. One such aid is diatomaceous earth. The tiny, single-celled diatoms in diatomaceous earth have very sharp exterior surfaces, much like coral. Diatomaceous earth works by abrasion. It pierces the waxy coating of an insect's body, compelling that body to exude its vital life fluids and therefore perish through dehydration. Unfortunately, diatomaceous earth does not work as well on hard-shelled adults. But it does a quite admirable job on fleas at the very vulnerable larval stage. If the larvae are killed, they will not pupate, and this means they cannot turn into adults. Sprinkle the white powder, *not aquarium diatomaceous crustations, which are used to filter water,* along all areas where larvae are likely to emerge. This means you must pay special attention to all areas where the animal rests and shakes himself off. Flea eggs fall off the dog and reside in crevices where he has shaken himself. Blood crumbs fall off also and become softened and rehydrated by the moisture in the air, enough to provide food for the voracious larvae.

Diatomaceous earth can be toxic to fish and birds, but is nontoxic to dogs and cats. Some suppliers of organic grain for human consumption are supposed to be either using or considering the widespread use of this substance as an alternative to more harmful chemicals used to help keep the bugs out of their grains. Some breeders use diatomaceous earth in their dogs' food for deworming. They have reported some success. However, we believe that continued internal use of diatomaceous earth can become detrimentally abrasive to the dog's delicate internal mucosa.

One herbal extraction which will kill the adult fleas quite well is rotenone, which is obtained from derris root. Pyrethrum is also an herbal extraction of a special strain of chrysanthemum, cultivated primarily in Kenya, Africa. Rotenone and pyrethrum work very well together as positive synergists in an inert base. Unfortunately, natural pyrethrum is in very short supply, and so some synthetic varieties classed as pyrethroids have been developed. These need further investigation to determine toxicity, but at least this is a move in the right direction. Pyrethrum alone only knocks the fleas down; fleas can and do recover. But with rotenone the effect is lethal. These natural substances can be even more severe in toxicity than some chemicals. But they are biodegradable. They do not remain to poison the atmosphere and every living thing for years to come. For severe area fumigation, sulfur candles, para crystals (mothballs), and burning cayenne pepper have all been used with success. All people and animals must be evacuated and the premises aired out for twenty-four hours afterwards. This can be used as a last resort or in critically infested areas.

There are other considerations in flea infestation. You must be mindful that heavy outdoor activity in a flea-infested area, where the dog is allowed hours of romping and rolling in grass and dirt, can also attract fleas onto your pet, and into the house. This is not to say that indoor confinement during the summer months is the answer. But if you have a pet that is sick with acute or chronic degenerative illness, then you must be even more careful not to add the often long-term stress of fleas to the already weakened animal.

Also consider how the flea problem can actually sometimes be compounded by the use of harsh flea-preventive shampoos, sprays, collars, tags, and other "helpful" preparations. These chemical concoctions often irritate and weaken the dog to a point where he begins scratching from the dermatitis, opens up lesions in the skin, and actually attracts fleas. Be sure to find a cooperative groomer who will use a mild, natural preparation of your choice, or at least your approval. You can use an olive-oil or coconut-oil-based shampoo or soap, with herbs added, to which you can also add some pure eucalyptus oils. Some herbalist groomers dip a flea comb in pure eucalyptus oil and comb through the animal, but we believe this oil is too concentrated and will irritate the dog's skin and respiration. If the groomer will not cooperate with your reasonable requests, then look elsewhere.

An alternative to having your dog groomed at a groomer's would be to hire an in-the-home groomer to perform the beauty services under your watchful eye. Try to find someone who has been personally recommended. One advantage of using an in-the-home groomer is that you can supervise the use of the correct shampoo. Also, the time of the entire procedure can be condensed into a few hours, instead of an all-day marathon. This has the very beneficial effect of minimizing the sometimes extreme stress on the animal, which could actually set him up as a prime candidate for flea problems. Many factors can induce stress in your dog and make him a nervous wreck. These factors include close proximity to strange people and strange barking or whining dogs, the smells of chemical hair sprays, flea sprays, shampoos, cigarette smoke, and noises such as talking, yelling, phones ringing, water running, and blowers drying. A substantial number of dogs and cats require tranquilization, because of the dire consequences.

A third approach to grooming your dog is to learn to do it yourself, so that you always have the option, should it become advantageous or necessary. In this way, you will learn to spot skin eruptions, tumors, and all manner of parasites before they get out of hand.

There are many seemingly unrelated health problems which can be induced through fleas. These include general irritability, an inability to concentrate, anemia, systemic toxemia, hot spots, allergies, ear, mange, and scabies mites (because fleas can transmit these other parasites from pet to pet), and flea vaccinia (because fleas penetrate skin and draw blood, they can transfer bacteria, viral filth, and blood parasites). Pets will also severely self-mutilate their flesh in an effort to stop the itching, thereby creating more serious secondary infections.

Because animals try to stop the itching by biting themselves, they sometimes swallow fleas. This leads to the problem of tapeworms. The tapeworm requires the flea as an intermediate host, in order to complete its life cycle. Most people have learned to recognize the familiar rice segments of the tapeworm in the animal's excrement. These segments are dry. When they are fresh, they undulate and each spews forth tiny eggs, also referred to as egg sacks. At this stage of activity, the tapeworm segments resemble cucumber seeds. Fleas in the larval or maggot (worm) stage can feed upon these tiny eggs. This allows the tapeworm to develop, along with the flea. When the animal swallows the flea, the tapeworm is released and then can attach itself to the intestines, thereby propagating a vicious cycle.

Tapeworms can be very difficult to get rid of using natural preparations. You can use a veterinary preparation such as Scoloban, which most of the time will get the scolex (head) of the tapeworm, but it has some disadvantages. Sometimes it does not work. Also, tape-

Illus. 104. The dog obeying the sit-stay command off the leash at the heel position.

Illus. 105. A moment for reflection. Love and praise are the rewards for work well done!

worms can reoccur during the next flea infestation or a continuing infestation. Sometimes these chemical taeniacides can cause severe gastrointestinal disorders and severe dehydration. If the problem returns, dosing the animal already weakened from the tapeworm with medication can have severe consequences.

What are our natural alternatives? Fortunately, tapeworm infestation is almost never a life-and-death matter. Most animals, including humans, live with a low level of infestation of one or several parasites. Sometimes the best we can do is to minimize the infestation naturally to as low a level as possible, while increasing the dog's vitality. Some foods and herbs that can be used in addition to the optimum food diet are garlic, onions, watercress, mustard greens, radishes, scallions, watermelon seeds, pumpkin seeds, wormwood, wormseed, rue, fennel, black walnut hulls, castor oil, senna pods, areca nuts, bear's-foot leaves, cucumber seeds, false unicorn, male fern, pinkroot, pomegranates, and self-heal. Treating any illness through natural means may be slower than we like, but we must persevere and, above all, have patience.

I hope we have shed some constructive light upon the flea problem. As you should well realize by now, there is no magic pill. But it is only by people understanding and recognizing all the factors involved in causing our pets to get sick that we can properly protect them. Industry should fervently research safer methods of controlling insects, to ensure responsibility not only to this generation but to all succeeding generations. And dog owners should understand and respect the symbiosis between host and parasite.

Growling

There is a saying that if a dog growls at you on Monday he will be biting you by Friday. What this really means is that growling leads to nipping, and then to biting. A growling dog is warning you that he doesn't like what you are doing and, if you continue, he is going to bite you.

If your dog is growling, it must be stopped before it progresses to biting. The way to stop it is to give this dog specific hard corrections, which consist of a jerk and release on the leash, every time he growls, and begin working him as described in the obedience section of this book. Growling must never be tolerated, and must always be corrected firmly. Growling dogs should never be hit.

Your dog may growl at other dogs, other animals, strangers, family members, or you. Growling is your dog's means of warning you or expressing worry, fear, or aggression. Dogs who never growl can display the behavior when you touch a part of their body that hurts them. For example, the dog's ear may have ulcerations, mite bites, wax buildup, or pus, so if the dog is touched on this painful part of his body, he will growl in self-defense. In such situations, when you treat the medical problem, the growling will stop. Perhaps a dog who has had his nails clipped at the groomer's suddenly starts to growl when you pet his feet. Did the groomer cut into the quick, hurt the paw, twist the leg, bruise the skin, or cut or burn his pads? Did he do anything unusual to cause this new behavior? Determine what occurred to make the dog growl and work slowly and deliberately to bring back his confidence and earn his trust again. These mishaps must not happen repeatedly or the dog will become very protective about that part of his body, with perhaps dire consequences for himself as well as persons unmindful of his unexpected and unexplained behavior.

Petting the face of an older dog could cause growling if he is starting to have teeth or eyesight problems. Gums can recede, get abscesses, have food or other material painfully caught between them, suffer from thermal sensitivity, or excess tartar can push up the gum lines. The eyes can be suffering from cataracts, glaucoma, allergic irritation, or a variety of other afflictions.

Not every growling problem needs a leash correction. But every growling problem should be dealt with constructively, whether that means removing the source of discomfort, using discipline, avoiding unfair or cruel behavior with your dog, or any combination thereof.

A dog who is growling may feel insecure in his surroundings and feel the need to control them. We need to build the dog's confidence and respect for us. Growling problems are best not handled as an abstract problem but as part of a larger picture of a sound and extensive relationship with your pet. If your dog has a severe growling problem which has not been resolved by the various methods you are using, do not hesitate to enlist the help of a professional.

Ineffective techniques or an inappropriate attitude can serve to make the problems worse. Too weak a correction or too fearful an attitude on your part, or too forceful a correction or heavy-handed an approach will prove counterproductive. The dog will always reveal to us through his body language what degree of praise is needed. But we have to read his body language correctly. If we do, we will solve the problem.

Jumping

Dogs can't understand why, when their owners come home, they can jump on them and be praised for it, but get scolded and yelled at for doing the same thing to strangers. Jumping dogs can be devastating to the person they jump on. Big dogs who jump can sometimes be dangerous to small children or infants.

Striking your dog with a knee lift into his chest may make your dog stop jumping on you, but it won't take him long to find out that your guests are not aware of this technique and, in the case of children and old people, are unable to execute it. The proper way to change your dog's attitude is with specific leash corrections, every time your dog attempts to jump on anyone; this will make him realize that jumping up is no longer going to be fun. Have him drag ten feet of clothesline when company is expected, and severely correct him every time he attempts to jump on anyone and praise him each time he stops. Consistent repetition will solve the problem. Remember, you can't reprimand him one day for jumping on your guests and then praise him the next for jumping on you. Consistency is most needed so that he will clearly learn, without confusion, what is expected of him.

Dogs have a primal urge to jump up and lick the mouth. As puppies, when they jump up and lick the mouth of mama dog, she regurgitates into their hungry little bodies. Even though this is a stage of puppyhood which most pet dogs never go through, they nevertheless instinctively know it is a good thing to find the mouth of mama or the surrogate mama.

Dogs also jump up to be petted, thinking they must reach to the sky to achieve this. Let your dog know that he can and will be petted if he stays on all fours. Enlist the help of your guests in doing this also. Don't just correct your dog when he jumps up. Reward him with praise for staying down.

Children love to tempt dogs to jump by pretending to throw Frisbees®, balls, or other toys. This behavior should be discouraged. Have your dog sit-stay before going out to retrieve something.

When you work your dog in basic obedience, the leash correction and the word NO will serve to reinforce the dragging-line correction given to your dog for jumping up on people. Be consistent, firm, and fair. Reward your dog for good behavior and clearly define to him with confidence and consistency what you expect, and all will change for the better.

Mounting Problems

If a male or female dog is mounting a person, the reaction is often to laugh because the behavior looks so outlandishly comical. This, of course, encourages the behavior and makes it more difficult, if not impossible, to control. It may seem funny to see your dog mounting the husband or wife in the family. But it is not amusing to witness this same sexual dominance behavior with a neighbor who is visiting or a child in the household.

The dog may be exhibiting this type of behavior because of a hormonal imbalance, or because he is trying to establish dominance. When a dog mounts another dog, it is affirming who is dominant (top dog). Some dogs will interchangeably contest the hierarchy by continually mounting each other, sometimes until a fight ensues. Others will mount and convince a submissive dog of their dominance, without further contest. Sometimes hormones are so out of balance in males or females as to cause serious behavior problems requiring medical adjustments. However, you should approach these problems *behaviorally* first, and make clear to the dog that mounting and sexually dominating anything in the household is not acceptable behavior. The obedience procedures described in this book will serve to convince your dog of the undesirability of this behavior. As with any other behavior, include obedience work with the NO correction. Issuing a firm NO correction on a leash or a dragging line and incorporating some of the obedience work (heeling, sitting, staying, downs, etc.) as necessary will reaffirm your dominance and control over your dog in any situation.

Running Away

The whole world is a very exciting place to a dog. It is as natural for the dog to want to explore all sights, smells, and sounds as it is for him to breathe. He sees life as a high-intensity adventure, and exploration is one of the greatest pleasures of a dog's life. So, don't be surprised if your dog disappears at every available opportunity.

Dogs are generally fearless and cautionless when embarking upon each new expedition. They haven't a clue as to what the word "safety" means. They also don't learn very well from cause and effect. A dog who was made sick by some rotting food outside or who has almost been hit by a car will almost certainly not understand this.

Family cooperation is essential when there is a dog that disappears at will. Everyone leaves it to someone else to watch the door to anticipate Rover's dash for the outdoors. He can zip across a living room in the blink of an eye and no one takes the blame.

Rover enjoys it when family members try to find him. The more they bellow and call for him, the more difficult it is to spot him. When he gets within eyesight of family members, he teases them mercilessly, dazzles one and all with his fancy footwork, and suckers them in for a chase. The family members play into Rover's hands

Illus. 106. Your dog should come out of the car *only when called.*

Illus. 107. In an emergency, your dog's memory of your severe corrections *can save his life!*

and find themselves chasing him down streets and across neighbors' lawns in an attempt to snare him. The family posse will eventually give up and limp dejectedly back home, where to their surprise Rover has arrived well before them, waiting patiently. He will ignore all profanities and warnings, probably already anticipating tomorrow's chase.

Does this scenario sound familiar? It happens to all too many families and their dogs. It is typical for some dogs to sneak past as you open the door and to escape out into the street. These dogs take the open door as a green light to visit the neighbors and buzz the neighborhood.

No matter how many times your dog has successfully run out the door, and no matter how old he is, you can, in approximately one minute, stop him from running out the door. To do this, you will need a choke collar with 15 feet of clothesline attached. Take your dog out of the room and have your helper prop the door open. Reenter the room with your dog, tightly clutching the line to your chest. Glance at your watch, take note of the time, and approach the door with your dog, ignoring him and his actions completely. As he starts running towards the door, silently make an about-turn and start running in the opposite direction. The impact should be timed to occur as the dog passes a few inches through the doorway. Immediately after the correction, still saying nothing to your dog, walk a few steps towards him, allowing slack to come into the line in case he attempts another charge out the door. If he does so, your reaction will be the same; silently turn and forcefully run in the opposite direction.

Most dogs will learn with one or two corrections; occasionally a dog will need three. No matter how many corrections a dog needs, your job is to provide them exactly as described above. If you do as instructed, you will soon see your dog standing at the threshold, looking out the open door, and looking back at you, as he refuses to go through the open door. The best way to teach a dog not to run out of an open doorway is *not* to make him sit and stay by the door, but to let him, when he is not under command, decide for himself that going through it alone is an unpleasant thing for him to do. As this positive conditioning is repeated, his attitude will change and going through an open door on his own will become something that he will soon discontinue.

Urinating

A dog may be urinating on the floor or carpet for a variety of reasons. He could be poorly trained and not be aware of the proper boundaries or the protocol for housebreaking. The dog may have been paper-trained in the house, and then the paper taken up with no constructive

alternative given to him. Now he will urinate on the area where he imagines the paper to be. Eventually, the entire floor becomes stained with urine and reeks of ammonia.

Let us question why Rover is piddling in the wrong place. We have clients who will claim that the dog is spitefully urinating when the urine overflows a stamp-size piece of paper they threw on the floor. When a dog is paper-trained, people rationalize that the dog should be able to hit the mark on a smaller and smaller target. I'd like to see them try that with their own toilet bowl! So, we need to ask, do we have the proper paper-training schedule, housebreaking schedule, or combination of both schedules?

If a complete and viable schedule has been set up for the dog, then let us question if we are giving too much fluid to the dog with not enough walks to process and relieve this intake. Does your dog drink a lot of water? If yes, check why. Does he drink more water in the hot weather, with certain foods, when nervous, or after walks, playing outside, or heavy exercise?

In some situations an increased thirst is perfectly normal. We must determine whether this increased drinking is normal or the dog is excessively thirsty. If the dog is excessively thirsty, then what is the psychological or physical reason for this? Once we have ruled out any physical reason, we then can question the behavioral aspects. Does the dog urinate slightly in many different areas, leaving a scent around the room? Is there another dog he is jealous of, another dog he would like to see gone? Is there a male dog in the house who has been there longer and over whom the younger one is trying to establish dominance, or vice versa?

Do you have a young, nervous dog or a dog with cystitis, inflammation of the urinary bladder? In cystitis, the normally acid urine becomes more alkaline. In this PH medium, bacteria which irritate and inflame the bladder wall and the opening can and do multiply. The dog's frequent urges to urinate can be accompanied by burning sensations. The dog tends to lick his genitals a lot, hoping to relieve some pressure and pain. The more the inflammation persists, the less the bladder is emptied.

Cystitis can become a chronic medical problem. Certain foods and not enough fluid can aggravate this terribly. Also, emotional stress can make it worse. You can't withhold water from a dog with cystitis.

Does your dog urinate on the floor shortly after you leave him home alone? Does this occur even though you walked him just before leaving? This may indicate he is anxious about being left alone. Has he been trained from puppyhood to handle some time alone, or has this been thrust upon him suddenly with overwhelming consequences? You will have to build up the time he is left alone gradually, and stick to the proper housebreaking schedule. Deodorize all areas with the proper solutions available at pet stores. Praise your dog upon your return for being good, and gradually lengthen and vary the time you are away.

Don't allow the dog free rein in the house whenever you are out, until he becomes more trustworthy. Gradually enlarge the area where the dog is left, but begin by leaving him in a kitchen or a kitchen and hallway. Hard tile floors are better than carpeted floors. Make leaving him alone a pleasant occurrence. Leave music on, and make sure it is not too hot or too noisy. Leave some chew toys scented with cheese, bacon, or chicken flavor for him as you leave. If dogs associate pleasant things happening to them when they are left alone they are less likely to become anxious.

Don't make the mistake of entering the house with anger, and, upon finding a puddle, punishing your dog. You will most definitely build even more anxiety, and worsen the problem. Praise your dog for not urinating and take him out right away to urinate; even if he has urinated in the house, take him out right away. Don't punish him after the fact. Then deodorize the area and try again.

Barking at Visitors

Dogs tend to pursue the mailman, the UPS person, all types of salespeople, and unwanted visitors with the fervor of a crazed maniac, even though they can be quite mild-mannered in other circumstances. Dogs usually bark incessantly, building up to a pitch and continuing for a while after the invader in question has long gone. Dogs can tear across the house, jumping from window to window to door, taking upon themselves the full responsibility of protecting the home. If it is a multi-dog household, the dogs who do not tend to be so protective at the door will nonetheless bark, since a chorus is always more effective than the lone call of one.

There is no way for the dog to know that the mailman, the UPS person, the salespeople, and the newspaper and circular men or women who appear at the door are simply doing their job. But, because the scenario repeats itself again and again, the dog's frenzy just builds and builds. Since the dog is usually the first to hear the interloper, he must make a great effort to make other members of the household aware of this threat.

What do the people in the household do when this occurs? The dog is chased out of the room, carted off to another corner of the house and confined behind closed doors, yelled and screamed at, or grabbed by the collar while the person deals with the business at hand—accepting the mail, getting the package, paying for the paper, accepting the circular.

In this typical scenario, the dog never gets to learn moderation or balance in his behavior. Most people get a dog to issue reliable warnings, so they don't want to discourage or eliminate the barking. It always comes in handy, and could even save a life some day. However, what do they do to *moderate* his behavior?

Once again, obedience training and the proper modification of behavior patterns can achieve the goal of getting your dog to issue moderate warning barks. Dogs must learn that warning barks are good, but excessive barking is undesirable and not necessary. He must be familiar with the basic structure in obedience training. If the dog has not learned to heel, sit, and stay when there are no distractions, how is he possibly going to sit and stay at the door peacefully, while you accept the mail, sign for a package, pay the paperboy, or take circulars or literature from a salesperson? The more convinced the dog is that you are in control, the less frenzied he will be.

You can best moderate your dog's behavior by showing him that you and he are a team, and as a team will attend the business at the door. You are both in control, and he is there to offer silent and subtle protection. The implication is that he can further react if the situation becomes necessary.

When your dog starts to bark furiously at the door, grab his dragging line and heel him to the door. Have him sit and stay as you open the door. Should he break the sit-stay, jerk his leash and utter the word NO and then, calmly, do the sit-stay again. Do this consistently until he obeys you. Enlist the cooperation of the person at the door. Most professional people are in a great hurry and not at all anxious to cooperate while you correct your dog. So, this is where friends and neighbors come in. Enlist their help to be the visitors at the door. The more this is practised, the better your dog will react when visitors appear.

Properly admit your friends or neighbors into the house and have them sit on a chair or the couch. Heel your dog into the room. Give the DOWN command, which should automatically by this point be a down-stay. After a few minutes, release the dog to say hello. If the dog sniffs, is civil, and walks away relaxed, taking his clue from you because you are relaxed, that's fine; if he is frenzied or pesky, use another down-stay for a few more minutes. Release him again and alternate this back and forth until you have the calm behavior you want. Remember, you must convince the dog that you are in control. When the friend or neighbor is ready to leave, it is a good idea to heel the dog off and make him sit and stay for the departure. If you control your visitor's entry and departure, your dog won't need to run amok.

Praise your dog for work well done. You are a team now. He reacts properly to your body posture and your tone of voice. When your dog barks, don't say NO. That means "I don't want you to do this." But you do want him to bark, just not excessively. When he gives a warning bark, say GOOD BOY, THAT'S ENOUGH, and proceed with the obedience routine. At some point, things will get easier, and you will have the best of both worlds. The mailman will be a lot happier, too!

It seems to be a strong conviction with many dogs that they should not like the mailman. No matter what it is that causes the dog's reaction—be it the uniform or the fact that the the mailman seems to be taking something from the house—anything more than a warning bark should not be tolerated. The answer to the problem lies within the pages of the obedience training section of this book. As you work on obedience, and as your dog improves, the mailman will become just another distraction for your well-trained dog to ignore as his attention remains focused upon you above all else.

Cast of Characters
Featured in This Book

Bill and Kathy are working together with Alex (at left), a Maltese, and Samantha, a mixed-breed dog. Alex and Samantha live together amicably. Maltese, although small, can be fearless, confident, and strong-willed. Samantha is so sweet and loving she gets along with all people and dogs.

Sigie is a beautiful, intelligent, and sweet Rottweiler who loves to work and play. Rottweilers are popular the world over as companion and protection dogs. Sigie is so obedient that he often appears with Bill and Kathy at demonstrations and in the obedience ring.

Bill Landesman's Dream is a national television star and one of the few attack-trained poodles in the country. Dream's ability to work at high levels of obedience training, do protection work, and be so loving and loyal a companion is a joy to reflect upon.

"Pete" is a beautiful, loving, mixed-breed dog with a tranquil personality. Being loved, fed, and walked are her favorite activities.

Mr. Pearlman is a borzoi or Russian wolfhound, also known as a Gentle Giant. He loves to go on long walks, to recline gracefully wherever he chooses, and to be stroked and petted endlessly.

Daisy, a yellow Labrador trained since puppyhood by Bill, demonstrates the most advanced off-leash work in our book. Because of the excellent follow-up training by her owners, she has reached the pinnacle of accomplishment in advanced obedience. Daisy and her owner frequently compete in the obedience ring.

Molly and Gertie, otherwise known as the Munchkins, are tiny Maltese terriers with a big heart and a repertoire of comedic talents. They love nothing better than to settle down in your lap together for an evening of petting and television.

Lady, Bill's mixed-breed dog, is a loving and loyal companion. Mixed breeds can do wonderful obedience training, and perform well in many dog show competitions.

Blaze is Kathy's fox terrier, who is "wired" for sound and is confident, alert, feisty, strong-willed, and very loving. Fox terriers are a lot of dog in a small package.

Kathy and Opieline, a black Chinese Shar-Pei. "Opie" has a confident and loving temperament and gets along with all people, dogs, and cats.

Ralph Kramden reposing with his bone. A Chinese Shar-Pei, he is protective without being aggressive. Shar-Pei can be wonderful working dogs.

Kathy and Bill. We got dressed up for this one. Dog trainers *can* feel comfortable in something other than dungarees. We both love our work and the many challenges we face dealing with dogs and their owners.

Acknowledgments

The authors wish to thank Charles Berman for his photographic excellence and his expertise in capturing shots that set this book far apart from most. His photography provides a wonderful supplement to the written text.

And special thanks to Karen, who gives us hope for the future with her sweetness, loyalty, and love.

Index